MW00638154

A Booze Hound's Guide To Gourmet

A Full Month of Starters, Main Courses and Desserts

Dedicated to My Lovely and Talented Assistant
The woman I happily cook for every day
My Wife - Mi-Kyoung Song

Dan McGuinness - A Booze Hound's Guide To Gourmet
Copyright © 2017 by Dan McGuinness
Design by Dan McGuinness
Printed in USA by Signature Book Printing
Forward by Pei Lin Yu
Poem by Rebecca Fitton
Edited by Jennifer Laing
Cover photo by Mi-Kyoung Song
A Red Hand Production, Santa Fe, NM
ISBN: 978-0-692-89108-7
www.boozehoundsguidetogourmet.com - where you can watch all of my "How To" videos

Foreword

As I write, it is Sunday: family dinner night at Dan and Mi-Kyoung's home. Their kitchen is aswirl with pots simmering, ovens baking, friends chopping, peeling, pouring wine, handing things out of the fridge. Conversation and laughter bubble and simmer, combining with the food ingredients into a delicious meal. Frequently, beginning with a few small subtle drops to a full blown Burn Down the House flambéed bananas – a river runs through it. Infused flavors of white wine and red wine, port and rum, vodka, gin, whiskey and my personal favorite, Sambuca (one of the most beautiful things in the world is a big bowl of cherry tomatoes sprinkled with tarragon leaves, glistening in a coating of Sambuca).

Savory, spicy, sweet, pungent, booze-inflected: is it the conversation? The food? Or the chef himself...? Many of the recipes in this book were developed when Dan was cooking on The Life of Riley - his charter yacht in the Bahamas and Virgin Islands. There is the feel of a journey in these delightful offerings, from small forays into appetizers, side dishes, entrées and desserts to longer, leisurely cruises through full dinners.

In A Booze Hound's Guide to Gourmet there is something for everyone, from a beginner intrigued by the idea of booze-infused cuisine, to a tired worker bee yearning for something delicious but not too hard to prepare, to an experienced cook in the mood for a little exploration and creativity (Painted Plates, anyone?)

As I type, the smells coming from the kitchen are becoming more delectable and compelling. Tonight the menu is Warm Spinach Salad, Balsamic-Braised Short Ribs, Mary's Onion Soup Potatoes, Truffle Baked Green Beans and a beautiful Kirschtorte. It's time to stop writing, jump up and set the table, pour a little wine and embark on our dinner journey together tonight, with friends from literally around the world. I hope you enjoy these journeys as much as we do. Bon appétit and cheers!

Pei-Lin Yu
July 16, 2017

Boozehound

Indulge in sumptuous and unforgettable sensations
Create juiciness, sensuality, delight
Dive deeply into the nuances of
Wine
    Spices
        Flavors
            Textures
              Aromas
                Bubbles
Cook as you have never cooked before

Eat as you have never eaten before
(unless you have been to Dan and Mi-Kyoung's house)
Eat slowly and savor the tastes
    Sweet
        Bitter
            Astringent
  Pungent
      Sour
          Salty
Witness the enjoyment of your guests
In their transcendent states
And know that these are the pleasures
Of the Boozehound

Rebecca Pott Fitton
July 27, 2017

A Booze Hound's Guide To Gourmet

I started writing this cookbook in the early fall of 1996. We had just left our charter yacht, The Life of Riley, in the Virgin Islands, in the care of someone with absolutely no interest in food. We were so intent on finding a suitable Captain to run the boat, that we totally missed having the "food talk" with his wife Sherry.

Our boat had quickly earned the reputation as the "food and wine" boat of the charter fleet in Nassau before we moved the boat to the Virgin Islands. It was my expectation that the same reputation would develop in St. Thomas.

I was aghast when Sherry called me just before their first charter and asked "so should I just slop whatever on their plates for dinner?" Horrified,and being someone who never followed or used others recipes, I immediately wrote down everything I could think of that I had lovingly prepared on the boat over the past 2 years.

The result was the first edition of this cookbook and was the closest thing to food direction that Sherry had back in 1996. For two years, she diligently followed the book and had copies printed and bound so that our guests could try their favorites at home.

It's interesting to note that the galley on the boat (the kitchen) had 12 square feet of floor space! Our current kitchen has over 200 square feet of floor space, four Wolf ovens, two large sink areas, three refrigeration spaces and an eight burner Wolf stove top - yet most of the recipes in this book were made on the boat back then.

Over the years, I have followed, adjusted, updated and added to my original collection of recipes that I sent down to Sherry in the Virgin Islands in 1996.

Throughout my almost 30 years of taking food very seriously, the one thing that has always bean a constant for me is the use of alcohol in my food - any type. From beer to wine to liquor to cordials - I always find some way to include booze in my food preparation.

Many of the recipes here are extremely simple. Gone are my days of preparing sauces from scratch - I learned a long time ago that a good prepackaged store-bought product tuned up with the right stuff is usually as good and often more stable than "from scratch" sauces. And, besides - it leaves more time for spending with your guests.

There are a small number of spirited liquids that will go a long way for everything from breakfast to dessert. I include these in my "Regular Must Have On Hand Supplies" before the recipes begin. You will find a small number of things regularly used for a large number of recipes. Contrary to "conventional wisdom" - I don't use good booze in food - the cheaper the better. Drink the good stuff - burn off the cheap stuff!

I am also very aware of gluten and lactose intolerance, so you will find many of these recipes specify gluten-free flour, or gluten-free pasta, or gluten-free bread, and a lot of cream or milk can be substituted with coconut or rice milk.

The format of this cookbook will help you make complete meals for a month – from starters, through main courses, to desserts. Many of the side items shown for a given meal will work perfectly with a number of other main items as shown in the pictures. I have intentionally used different sides in the photos, than shown in some of the recipes. I also include a Time Line for all of the components of the main courses, a Total Time to make each entrée and a Degree of Difficulty for all items, with 1/4 being the easiest and 4/4 the most difficult. Most Items in this cookbook are 1/4, so please do not be intimidated.

As a serious foodie, I have found that my happiest time is when I am in the kitchen, cooking for those that are an important part of my life.

Don't be afraid to experiment. You will do best using this as much as a guide for ideas, rather than a rigid, must follow, recipe book. And if you think any recipe (from anywhere) needs more or less of something - change it to your taste!

Remember – "it's only food!"

Enjoy!

Regular Must Have On Hand Supplies

Pantry:
Flour: all purpose and gluten-free
Cream of tartar
Baking powder - I usually add to gluten-free flour
Sugars: white, brown and powdered
Agave syrup or honey
Cocoa powder
White chocolate (chips are fine)
Semi-sweet chocolate
Bitter chocolate
Vinegars: balsamic, red wine, raspberry and white
Oils: olive, vegetable, sesame, truffle
Coconut milk
Coco Lopez (sweetened cream of coconut)
Rice: arborio, wild, white and brown
Quinoa
Pasta: various types, including orzo
Sesame seeds: black and regular
Pine nuts
Nuts: peanuts, almonds, walnuts - and any other nuts you enjoy.
Bottled dressings and packaged sauces: Knorr, Briannas,
       Asian fish sauce, low sodium and regular soy sauce,
       spicy Thai sweet chili sauce

In the fridge:
Butter - unsalted - lots!
Heavy or whipping cream - (35% fat)
Half & Half - (or mix heavy/whipping cream with water)
Hard cheese: Parmesan, Asiago, Romano, Robusto
Soft cheese: Brie, Mozzarella, Ricotta, Blue
New Mexico roasted green chili

Vegetable bin:
Ginger
Garlic
Onions
Shallots
Scallions
Leeks
Potatoes
Sweet potatoes
Lemons and limes

Spices:
Coarse salt
Peppercorns
Pure vanilla extract
Ground ginger

Cloves
Cinnamon: ground and sticks
Nutmeg: ground and whole nuts (need a grater for nuts)
Rosemary
Tarragon
Basil
Mint
New Mexico red chili powder
Curry paste and powder

Booze:
Port - cheap
Red wine - cheap - jug or box
White wine - cheap - jug or box
Bubbly - cheap sparkling or prosecco
Grand Marnier - or any cheap orange liqueur
Frangelico
Vodka
Dark rum
Light rum
Brandy - the cheapest jug
Tequila
Sambuca

Equipment:
Knives: from paring to at least an 8" Chef's (and sharpener)
Stainless bowls: lots - from small to big
Plates: different sizes and shapes for different courses
Ramekins and custard cups
Oven-proof dishes, casseroles, and metal pans with racks
Saucepans, pots and frying pans - various sizes (and lids)
Insta-read meat thermometer
Baking sheets - as large as will fit in your oven
Whip-it whip creamer and CO2 cartridges
Butcher elastic mesh or string
Parchment paper
Tinfoil
Pastry brush
Shaker for powdered sugar, cocoa, cinnamon, red chili
       powder etc.
Zester
Salad spinner
Metal sieve or China cap
Blender or food processor
Electric mixer

A Booze Hound's Guide to Gourmet
Recipe Index

STARTERS

SALADS

SOUP

SPECIAL AND DIFFERENT APPETIZERS

MAIN COURSES

MEAT

Coconut Crusted Rack of Lamb --- 32
w/Marsala Mint Sabayon, Sweet Potatoes w/Lentils and Sweet & Sour Red Cabbage

Stuffed Pork Tenderloin ------------------------------------- *Ruth and Ernst Luthi* ------------- 34
w/Apricot Bacon Brandy Stuffing and Sauce, Saffron Risotto and Baked Cheesy Asparagus

Jimmy's Cinnamon Red Chili Beef Tenderloin Steaks ----------- *Jimmy McGuinness* -------------- 36
w/Green Chili Hollandaise, Port Mushrooms, Baked Sweet Potato Fries and Garlic Broccoli

Veal Osso Buco --- 38
w/Crispy Fried Leeks, Polenta and Roasted Root Vegetables

Balsamic Braised Short Ribs -- *(Seattle Times)* ------------------ 40
w/Mary's Onion Soup Potatoes and Truffle Steamed Green Beans

Elk Tenderloin --- 42
w/Gin Juniper Sauce, Chipotle Coconut Scalloped Sweet Potatoes and Sambuca Tarragon Cherry Tomatoes

Pork Tenderloin -- 44
w/Soy Maple Brandy Sauce, Sambuca Oyster Mushroom Quinoa and Eggplant Timbales

Meatloaf --- 46
w/Port Mushrooms, Asiago Mashed Potatoes and Truffle Baked Green Beans

Herbed Veal Chops --- 48
w/Mashed Cauliflower, Brussels Sprout "Fluff" and Burnt Cherry Rum Shishito Peppers

Double Thick Pork Chop -- 50
w/Hoisin Black Bean Brandy Marinade/Sauce, Lundberg Countrywild Rice and Garlic Broccoli and Fennel

Marinated Flank Steak --- 52
w/Port Mushrooms, Mashed Sweet Potatoes and Carrots Vichy

POULTRY

Spicy Grilled Chicken -- 54
w/Baked Potatoes and Grilled Mixed Vegetables

Stacked Chicken Breast (*Topped w/Eggplant, Chevre and Pesto*) ------------------------- ----------- 56
w/Rossa Risotto and Sesame Steamed Snow Peas

Stuffed Chicken Breast (*Stuffed With Prosciutto, Spinach and Swiss Cheese*) ----------------------- 58
w/Grand Marnier Cream Sauce, Garlic Sage Roasted Fingerling Potatoes and Tofu Snap Peas

Boneless Stuffed Cornish Hens -- 60
w/Lobster Risotto and Steamed Broccoli

Turducken - (*Boned and Stuffed, Turkey, Duck and Chicken*) -------------------------------------- 62
w/Oyster Bourbon Cornbread Stuffing, Dirty Mashed Potatoes and Carrots

Duck Breast (*w/Chinese 4 Spice*) --- 64
w/Raspberry Port Sauce, Jasmine Rice, and Sesame Grilled Asparagus

FISH

Seabass Mariscada (*A One Pot Dinner For 4*) --- 66

Grilled Mahi-Mahi --- 68
w/Tequila Jalapeño Cilantro Glaze, Baked Sweet Potato Fries and Roasted Truffle Brussels Sprout

Grilled Seabass --- 70
w/Hoisin Black Bean Brandy, Lundberg Countrywild Rice, Steamed Asparagus and Crispy Fried Leeks

Seafood en Papillote (*Baked in a Paper Bag*) --- 72
w/Salmon, Shrimp, Scallops, Mushrooms, Broccoli, Potatoes, Carrots, Champagne Cream Sauce and Caviar

Stuffed Grouper (*Bacon Wrapped, Mushroom and Crab Stuffed*) ------------------------------------ 74
w/Dill Hollandaise Sauce, Sambuca Oyster Mushroom Risotto, and Baked Green Beans

Potato Crusted Salmon Fillet --- 76
w/Grilled Sesame Brussels Sprouts and Truffled Corn

General Hints, Tips and Suggestions

Booze. Obviously the theme of this cookbook is cooking with booze, and while that has been a big part of my cooking style, I know there are many who simply cannot go this route. Please don't pass on these recipes because of the alcohol content. Keep in mind that in most cases the alcohol is burned off or cooked out while still retaining the flavor. That being said, I always accommodate a request for alcohol-free at home. Most of these recipes will work fine and still taste great if you substitute the alcohol for some other flavored liquid - different vegetable or fruit stocks or juices will give good results.

Wine Pairing Suggestions. Admittedly, my wine preference runs almost exclusively to the US west coast reds. I love Napa Cabs, Sonoma Zins, Washington Syrahs, anything from Ridge, Silver Oak, Heitz, Quilceda and Paloma! I always think the best wine for everything is RED! Because of my skewed preferences, I have asked Roland Hankerson, of JJ Buckley Fine Wines, to suggest wine pairings for each main course, in 3 price ranges - $15, $25, $50 all + . I did sneak in some favorites though!

Gluten-free and dairy-free. Most of these recipes can be prepared with gluten-free flour, or gluten-free pasta, or gluten-free bread. As well, most times you can substitute milk, cream, or Half & Half with coconut milk or rice milk.

Cooking techniques can sound intimidating or confusing, but they're not. Here are a few of the techniques I refer to:

whisk – to mix or combine ingredients with a whisk

purée – in a food processor – to blend until smooth

reserve – to set aside for later use

sauté – using a very hot pan and a small amount of fat to cook the food very quickly - this will brown the food's surface and develop complex flavors

sweat – this is the gentle heating of vegetables in a small amount of fat, stirred and turned over frequently, so any emitted liquid will evaporate

reduce – to continue cooking or heating or boiling until the volume is lessened - thin liquids can be reduced to a thick(er) consistency with heat and time - basically the liquid boils off leaving a lesser, more solid volume

bain – a cooking method where the item is placed in a baking pan of water in the oven - the cooking happens when the water bath ("bain") boils - this method also prevents the bottom of the food container from burning or drying out

Salt and Pepper. Very rarely do I salt anything I am cooking, but always the water for boiling anything. However, salt and pepper to taste means your and your guest's taste.

Garlic. I love garlic. I always use more than what is shown here. The amounts shown are a good starting point. Experiment...

Leftovers. A number of the recipes here will yield more than will be used for a particular meal. Most, if not all of the sauces, glazes, dressings and dinner courses do very well being refrigerated for later use. If in doubt - use the smell test - if it smells bad - don't eat it.

Canned or Fresh. I often specify canned, frozen or pre-packaged fruit or vegetables. This is usually because the recipe started on the boat and I had to store these items long term. I couldn't just run out to the store when I was anchored in a secluded bay. In almost all cases you can easily substitute canned for fresh.

Lettuce. I usually specify a particular lettuce for these salads. Please feel free to substitute what you like, or what is available for any of them.

Cheese. You will see that I offer different options when I use cheese - usually I will interchange cheese based on what I have, or what a guest may prefer. You can interchange hard cheeses like Parmesan, Romano, or Asiago, just as you can usually interchange soft cheeses like Brie, cream cheese, blue cheese, or mascarpone. Again, don't be afraid to experiment – if you like a different cheese than I call for, use it!

Fat. You can usually interchange butter, olive oil, vegetable oil or even exotic fats like bone marrow, or my favorite - the leftover fat from searing foie gras! I have a container in my fridge labeled "foie." I use it in place of olive oil for risotto all the time.

Asparagus. I have found the best way to clean and prep asparagus is to snap the woody end off at the natural breaking point. Hold the ends of a piece of asparagus in each hand and gently bend. It will snap off at the natural breaking point. You could keep the woody ends for stock.

Craisins. These are also known as dried cranberries.

Oils. I always use flavored oils. My favorite is truffle oil, but try different ones.

Reduced Balsamic. This is one of the most versatile garnishes. Pour a bottle of balsamic vinegar in a large saucepan and bring to a boil uncovered. Continue boiling until the volume is reduced to about a third. Remove from the heat and when slightly cooled, pour this thickened reduction into a squeeze bottle. Refrigerate and slightly reheat in the microwave for use. This will last forever in the refrigerator.

Heavy/Whipping Cream. Any cream with at least 35% fat is heavy or whipping cream. The terms heavy and whipping can be used interchangeably, and both are whippable.

Flaring Green Onions. Green onions or scallions can make a great garnish by cleaning the whole onion and the cutting the base of the bulb off. Then slice the bottom 2" or so (closest to the bulb) with long cuts - maybe 4 or 6. Place the cleaned and trimmed onion in iced water and the sliced ends will "flare."

Fish. Don't be afraid to use different fish in these recipes. Most firm white fish can be changed for seabass, or grouper, cod, tilapia or mahi-mahi. Experiment and try other fish than what is called for.

Cleaning Peppers. I use a lot of bell type peppers. When I refer to "cleaning" them, I mean cut them in half - long way, cut out the stem and other end, and remove all seeds and seed membrane, and then cut the pepper as called for in the recipe.

Baking and cooking at elevation. I am in Santa Fe, New Mexico. We are at about 7,000 feet of elevation. Food cooks and bakes differently than in the Caribbean at sea level. At elevation, the air pressure is lower, so foods take longer to cook. Temperatures and/or cook times may need to be adjusted. Water boils at a lower temperature, so foods prepared with water (such as pastas and soups) may take longer to cook. Here are some good guidelines from King Arthur Flour:
Oven temperature - Increase 15 to 25° - use the lower increase when making chocolate or delicate cakes.
Baking time - Decrease by 5-8 min. per 30 min. of baking time.
Sugar - Decrease by 1 tablespoon per cup.
Liquid - Increase by 1 to 2 tablespoons at 3,000 feet. Increase by 1½ teaspoons for each additional 1,000 feet. You can also use extra eggs as part of this liquid, depending on the recipe.
Flour- At 3,500 feet, add 1 more tablespoon per recipe. For each additional 1,500 feet, add one more tablespoon.

Abbreviations. Tbsp. = tablespoon(s), tsp. = teaspoon(s), C. = cup(s), lb. = pound(s), oz. = ounce(s), min. = minute(s), hr. = hour(s), qt. = quart(s)

Doneness of Meat. red meat - rare 125°, medium-rare 135°, medium 145°, medium-well 150°, well 160°, chicken 160°+, pork 145°+-, fish 140°-145°

Recipe conversion - standard/metric. The following apps will help convert to metric and scaling up or down: *iPhone* - www. kitchencalculator.net/ - *Android* - https://play.google.com/store/apps/details?id=com.redbinary.rmc&hl=en

The Life of Riley - 55' Cheoy Lee Motor Yacht - Virgin Gorda, BVI, 2004 - My home and kitchen from 1994 - 2009

Caesar Salad

Time To Prepare and Tips
Total Prep, Mix, Assemble, Plate time - 15 min.
Dressing can be prepared ahead and refrigerated until needed - will last refrigerated for weeks
Dressing recipe can also be doubled or more and refrigerated for easy, fast, future use

Serves - 4

Caesar Dressing
4 garlic cloves - peeled
6 Tbsp. olive oil
2-3 Tbsp. lemon juice
1 tsp. hot pepper sauce
1 Tbsp. Dijon mustard
1 tsp. Worcestershire sauce
1 Tbsp. mayonnaise
black pepper to taste

Caesar Dressing...cont.
1 Tbsp. horseradish
6-8 Tbsp. Parmesan cheese or other hard Italian cheese - grated or shredded
          use half of cheese for dressing - save half for garnish when plated
          anchovies or anchovy paste and capers - to taste

romaine lettuce for 4 - cleaned, washed, torn into bite size pieces, spun dry

Caesar Dressing
Blend all dressing ingredients until smooth

Add capers and anchovy to blended dressing - to taste

Refrigerate until needed

Assembly and Plating
Either add dressing to lettuce, mix and plate

   or -

Plate lettuce and pour dressing over lettuce

In either case, place salad centered on each plate

Garnish
Top completed salad with additional grated cheese

Caesar Salad with Shaved Parmesan Cheese

Spinach Salad

Time To Prepare and Tips
Total Prep, Mix, Assemble, Plate time - 45 min.
Dressing can be prepared ahead and refrigerated
Reheat when needed

Serves - 4

Dressing
½ lb. bacon - cut into 1" pieces - fried until crisp - reserve grease
2 Tbsp. Dijon mustard
2 Tbsp. honey or agave
2 Tbsp. Grand Marnier or other orange liqueur
1 - 14 oz. can mandarin oranges - strained - reserve juice
1 red bell pepper - cleaned and cut into small pieces

Spinach Salad
spinach for 4 - cleaned, washed, cut into bite size pieces and spun dry

2 hard boiled eggs - crumbled
½ lb. button mushrooms - cleaned, stemmed and sliced thin

Dressing (5 min. prior to serving)
Re-heat 2-3 Tbsp. of bacon grease

Add 2 Tbsp. Dijon

Add 2 Tbsp. honey or agave

Add 2 Tbsp. Grand Marnier or other orange liqueur

Add 1 Tbsp. mandarin orange juice

Bring to boil

Add red peppers and heat 3 min.

Remove from heat

Spinach Salad
In salad bowl combine: spinach, bacon, oranges, crumbled hard
        boiled eggs, red and sliced mushrooms

Pour hot dressing over salad and mix well

Plate
Place salad centered on each plate, and serve quickly so salad is
        warm when served

*Spinach Salad with a Warm Grand Marnier, Bacon, Dijon,
Mushroom, Red Pepper Dressing*

Pear Avocado Walnut Salad

Time To Prepare and Tips
Total Prep, Mix, Assemble, Plate time - 15 min.
Dressing can be prepared ahead and refrigerated until needed.

Serves - 4

Dressing
2 Tbsp. walnut oil
1 Tbsp. pear juice - from can of pears
2-3 Tbsp. raspberry vinegar
salt and pepper to taste

Pear Avocado Walnut Salad
mixed lettuce greens for 4 (and red lettuce if available) - cleaned, washed, spun dry

1 - 15 oz. can sliced pears - reserve juice and slice pears thinner
2 ripe avocados - skin avocados and sliced thin

Garnish
½ C. walnuts - chopped
black sesame seeds

Dressing
Combine all dressing ingredients and whisk

Plate
Place mixed lettuce centered on each plate

Alternate and overlap slices of pear/avocado/pear etc. around bottom section of plate

Re-whisk dressing and pour over lettuce and pear/avocado fan

Garnish
Lightly sprinkle walnuts over everything

Sprinkle black sesame seeds around plate

Pear Avocado Walnut Salad

Caprese Salad

Time To Prepare and Tips
Total Prep, Mix, Assemble, Plate time - 30 min.
This can be made ahead and refrigerated

Serves - 4

Dressing
½ C. olive oil
¾ C. balsamic vinegar
1 package or bunch or basil leaves - (dried will work in a pinch)
salt and pepper to taste

Caprese Salad
2-3 very ripe red tomatoes - sliced ¼" thick
¼-½ lb. either mozzarella cheese sliced or chevre crumbled

Garnish
fresh basil - snipped into small pieces or dried if fresh not available

Caprese Salad
Arrange a layer of sliced tomatoes to cover bottom of glass pie
    plate

Salt and pepper tomatoes to taste

Pour ⅓ of oil and balsamic mixture over tomatoes

Sprinkle with fresh basil - cut leaves into small pieces and scatter
    over tomato layer - (if using dried basil liberally sprinkle)

Place pieces of cheese on each tomato slice

Repeat above process with remaining tomatoes and cheese

Pour any remaining oil and balsamic on top of tomato/cheese/
    basil

Plate
With slotted spoon or spatula - divide tomatoes among plates

Make sure cheese is distributed among tomatoes

Garnish
Sprinkle plate with fresh basil snips

Caprese Salad of Ripe Tomatoes, Chevre and Olive Oil,
Balsamic Vinegar and Basil

Mango Salad (perfect with Thai dinner on pg 84)

Time To Prepare and Tips
Total Prep, Mix, Assemble, Plate time - 30 min. or less
Dressing can be prepared ahead and refrigerated until needed

Serves - 4

Dressing
2 tsp. fish sauce
¼ C. sesame oil
¼ C. rice wine vinegar

Garnish
½ C. chopped peanuts
1 Tbsp. black sesame seeds

Mango Salad
1 green mango - skinned, pitted and julienned
1 ripe mango - skinned, pitted and julienned
1 red onion -peeled and julienned
1 green apple - skinned, seeded and julienned
1 handful of bean sprouts
½ yellow bell pepper - cleaned and julienned
1 red bell pepper - cleaned and julienned

½ head Boston or bib lettuce

Dressing
Combine all dressing ingredients and whisk

Mango Salad
Combine all salad ingredients EXCEPT the Boston or bib
    lettuce and toss in large bowl

Add dressing to salad ingredients EXCEPT the Boston or Bib
    lettuce

Plate
On each plate place a couple of lettuce leaves to form a base or bed

Plate dressed mixed salad on top of lettuce bed

Garnish
Sprinkle chopped peanuts and black sesame seeds over salad

Mango Salad

Arugula Salad, w/Toasted Pine Nuts, Craisins, Chevre

Time To Prepare and Tips
Total Prep, Mix, Assemble, Plate time - 15 min. or less
Definitely one of the easiest, fastest, "everyone's favorite" salad you can make! If you have raw pine nuts, toast them in a dry hot pan

Serves - 4

Dressing
Briannas Blush Wine Vinaigrette Dressing

Arugula Salad
arugula for 4 - cleaned, washed, spun dry

1 C. toasted pine nuts
1 C. Craisins
4 oz. crumbled chevre cheese

Arugula Salad
Combine all salad ingredients and toss
        with Briannas Blush Wine Vinaigrette
        Dressing

Plate
Place mixed salad centered on each plate

Briannas Blush Wine Vinaigrette Dressing

Arugula Salad, w/Toasted Pine Nuts, Craisins, Chevre and Briannas Blush Wine Vinaigrette Dressing

Greek Salad

Time To Prepare and Tips
Total Prep, Mix, Assemble, Plate time - 30 min.
Dressing can be prepared ahead and refrigerated

Serves - 4

Dressing
¼ C. olive oil
¼ C. raspberry vinegar
2 tsp. oregano dried or 1 Tbsp. fresh
sugar to taste
salt and pepper to taste

Greek Salad
1 cucumber - peeled, seeded and cubed ½"
1 red bell pepper - cleaned and cubed ½"
1 green bell pepper - cleaned and cubed ½"
2 tomatoes - cleaned and cubed ½"
1 red onion - peeled and sliced
1½ C. feta cheese - crumbled in bigger chunks
½-1 - 10-12 oz. can black olives - sliced

Dressing
Combine all dressing ingredients and whisk

Greek Salad
Combine all salad ingredients
Pour mixed dressing ingredients over salad and let sit prior
        to serving

Plate
Re-toss immediately and place salad centered on each plate

Greek Salad

Fennel, Prawn and Citrus Salad - *Jennifer Laing*

Time To Prepare and Tips
Total Prep, Mix, Assemble, Plate time - 30 min.
You can use shrimp in place of prawns and pink grapefruit in place of pomello - same prep

Serves - 4

Dressing
½ C. torn mint leaves
¼ C. fresh orange juice
¼ C. dry white wine
¼ C. olive oil
2 Tbsp. red wine vinegar
salt and pepper to taste

Fennel, Prawn and Citrus Salad
1 large fennel head - finely sliced
24 medium prawns (or shrimp) - cooked and peeled
3 inner stalks celery - sliced
4 kumquats - sliced and seeded
1 pomello - peeled, de-membraned and segmented

Dressing
Combine all dressing ingredients and whisk

Fennel, Prawn and Citrus Salad
Keep sliced fennel in iced water while preparing other
    ingredients

In a large bowl add mixed dressing ingredients and all salad
    ingredients except fennel

Drain fennel and add to all other ingredients

Toss to combine and season to taste

Plate
Place salad centered on each plate

Serve immediately, with sliced baguette and butter if desired

Fennel, Prawn and Citrus Salad

Mixed Greens with Ernst's Grilled Orange and Bourbon Salmon - *Ruth and Ernst Luthi*

Time To Prepare and Tips
Total Prep, Marinate (90 min.)
Bake 15 min.+- Assemble 15 min.
Total time - 2 hr.
(can marinate ahead of time and save 90 min. at serving time)

Serves - 4

Salmon
¼ C. bourbon
¼ C. fresh orange juice
¼ C. low sodium soy sauce (Tamari for gluten free)
¼ C. packed brown sugar
¼ C. chopped green onions
3 Tbsp. chopped fresh chives
2 Tbsp. fresh lemon juice
2 garlic cloves - peeled and chopped
4 small salmon fillets (about 1" thick) 4 oz.+-
cooking spray

Salad
mixed greens for 4 - cleaned, washed, torn into bite size pieces, spun dry

Dressing
½ C. olive oil
¾ C. balsamic vinegar - (can use any fancy vinegar if desired)

Salmon
Combine first 8 Salmon ingredients in a large ziploc plastic bag

Add salmon

Seal and marinate in refrigerator 1½ hr. turning bag occasionally

Prepare grill or broiler

Remove salmon from bag, reserving marinade

Place salmon on a grill rack or broiler pan coated with cooking
    spray

Cook 6 min. on each side or until fish flakes easily when tested
    with a fork, basting frequently with reserved marinade

Salmon Marinade Sauce
Reduce marinade over medium heat

Put marinade through sieve and cook down to a thick sauce
    consistency

Plate
Toss mixed greens with dressing ingredients

Place mixed lettuce centered on each plate

Top greens with piece of salmon

Top salmon with reduced marinade sauce

Mixed Greens with Ernst's Grilled Orange and Bourbon Salmon

Butternut Squash Salad

Time To Prepare and Tips
Prep 15 min.
Squash Baking 1 hr. Cooling 1 hr. (squash can be prepared and refrigerated for up to 24 hr. ahead)
Assembly 10 min.
Total time - 2 hr. 30 min. - if squash is done ahead of time, this salad can be put together less than 30 min. ahead of serving
The salad tastes best if made ahead and allowed to rest for at least 2 hr.

Serves - 4

Dressing
½ C. tarragon vinegar
¼ C. olive oil
3 Tbsp. honey
2 Tbsp. Dijon mustard
2 garlic cloves - peeled and minced
½ tsp. salt
½ tsp. dried basil
½ tsp. dried tarragon
freshly ground black pepper

Butternut Squash Salad
1 butternut squash
1 red bell pepper - cleaned and cut into ½" cubes
1 green bell pepper - cleaned and cut into ½" cubes
1 red onion - peeled and coarsely chopped
¼ C. fresh parsley - chopped

Butternut Squash Salad
Preheat the oven to 375°

Coat the bottom of a 13" x 9" x 2" deep pan with nonstick cooking
spray and set aside

Cut the stem and bottom of the squash, halve and scoop out the
seeds, peel the squash and cut into 1" to 1½" pieces

Place squash pieces in prepared baking pan and cook for 45 min.
to 1 hr. or until tender but not mushy

Allow to cool

Place cooled squash in a large bowl

Add the peppers, onion - and parsley

Dressing
Mix dressing ingredients and whisk vigorously

Assembly
Pour dressing over squash and pepper mixture, toss well to coat

Refrigerate before serving

Plate
Place salad centered on each plate

Butternut Squash Salad

Spinach, Red Onion and Andouille Salad

Time To Prepare and Tips
Prep 10 min.
Cook onion and andouille 20 min.
Assembly 5 min.
Total time - 30-40 min.+-

Serves - 4

Dressing
½ C. olive oil
¾ C. balsamic vinegar

Spinach, Red Onion and Andouille Salad
spinach for 4 - cleaned, washed, torn into bite size pieces, spun dry

1 red onion - peeled and sliced thin
3 andouille sausages diced - ¼"-½" dice

Dressing
In a large saucepan combine olive oil and balsamic vinegar

Add sliced red onion and diced andouille sausage

Bring to boil and continue to cook for 10 min.

Spinach, Red Onion and Andouille Salad
Place washed spinach in heat proof bowl

Pour hot oil/vinegar, cooked andouille sausage and red onion
    slices over spinach

If the dressed salad appears too wet - don't be afraid to strain
    the excess dressing out

Plate
Place salad centered on each plate

This should be served warm

Spinach Salad with Red Onion Andouille Sausage,
Olive Oil and Balsamic Vinegar

Broccoli Salad

Time To Prepare and Tips
Prep 15 min
Fry bacon 15 min.
Assembly 10 min.
Total time - 45 min.+-

Serves - 4

Dressing
¼ C. brown sugar
2 Tbsp. white vinegar
¼ C. mayonnaise (Miracle Whip)
A pinch dry mustard
salt and pepper to taste

Broccoli Salad
10 strips bacon - cooked and crumbled
2 heads broccoli - cut into bite sized pieces and blanched (or raw)
¾ C. red onion - peeled and chopped
1 C. toasted pine nuts
1 small container cherry or plum tomatoes - cut in half

Dressing
Combine all dressing ingredients and whisk

Broccoli Salad
Combine all salad ingredients and toss with dressing

Refrigerate at least 2 hr. before serving - longer is better

Plate
Place salad centered on each plate

Broccoli Salad

Fennel, Cucumber Salad - *Ruth and Ernst Luthi*

Time To Prepare and Tips
Prep 15 min.
Dressing mix 5 min.
Total time - less than 30 min.

Serves - 4

Dressing
4 oz. yogurt
1 Tbsp. mayonnaise
1-1½ Tbsp. lemon juice
salt, pepper and cayenne to taste

Fennel, Cucumber Salad
1 fennel bulb - white part cut into thin slices
2 large cucumbers - peeled, seeded - cut into thin slices
1 Tbsp. parsley
1 Tbsp. dill
½ C. sliced black olives

Garnish
2 hardboiled eggs - cut into ⅛ wedges

Dressing
Combine all dressing ingredients and whisk

Fennel, Cucumber Salad
Mix fennel and cucumbers

Add dressing

Add parsley and dill to taste

Add black olives

Season to taste

Plate
Place salad centered on each plate

Garnish
Place hard-boiled egg wedges around the plate

Fennel Cucumber Salad

Warm Breast of Duck and Pear Salad

Time To Prepare and Tips
Prep and marinate duck 45 min. Cook duck 30 min. Duck can be prepped, cooked and refrigerated up to 24 hr. ahead -
(slice cooked duck at the last minute)
Coulis 30 min. (while duck cooks) Total time - 1 hr. 30 min.
Chinese 4 spice mixture is equal parts - cinnamon, white pepper, ginger, nutmeg - at least 1 tsp. each
Fresh pears can always be substituted for canned

Serves - 4

Duck
1 duck breast duck
2 Tbsp. Chinese 4 spice mixture
1 C. port

Salad
mixed lettuce greens (and red lettuce if available) for 4 - cleaned, washed, spun dry

1 - 15 oz. can sliced pears - reserve juice and slice pears thinner

Coulis
1 C. white vinegar
1 - 10-12 oz. package frozen raspberries - thawed
sugar to taste
salt and pepper to taste

Garnish
½ C. chopped walnuts
½ C. fresh raspberries

Duck
Preheat oven to 350°

Score duck fat in hash X marks - just through the fat

Rub duck with 4 spice mix all over

Pour port into bottom of baking dish

Place 4 spice rubbed duck into port - fat side down for 30 min.

Remove duck from port - reserve port - pat duck dry

Bake duck at 350° for 30 min. on a rack - fat side down

Remove from heat and rest 15 min. prior to slicing

Slice cooked duck very thin (you can keep fat on duck if desired)

Coulis
Combine marinade, vinegar and thawed berries

Heat and reduce to thin sauce consistency

Sweeten with sugar or reserved pear juice to taste

Strain and reserve

Plate
Place mixed lettuce centered on each plate

Alternate and overlap slices of pear/duck/pear etc. around bottom section of plate

Whisk strained coulis and pour over lettuce and pear/duck fan

Garnish
Lightly sprinkle walnuts over everything

Place several raspberries on plate

Warm Breast of Duck and Pear Salad

Spinach, Walnut and Blue Cheese Salad

Time To Prepare and Tips
Toast walnuts 15 min.
Assembly 5 min.
Total time - less than 30 min.

Serves - 4

Dressing
Briannas Poppy Seed Dressing

Spinach, Walnut and Blue Cheese Salad
baby spinach for 4 - cleaned, washed, spun dry

Spinach, Walnut and Blue Cheese Salad...cont.
1 C. toasted walnuts
4 oz. crumbled blue cheese
Garnish
½ C. toasted walnuts - chopped

Spinach, Walnut and Blue Cheese Salad
Combine all salad ingredients and toss
with Briannas Poppy Seed Dressing

Plate
Place salad centered on each plate

Garnish
Scatter small toasted walnut pieces over
top of salad

Briannas Poppy Seed
Dressing

Spinach, Walnut and Blue Cheese Salad

Four Squash Soup with a Wiggly Man

Time To Prepare and Tips
Squash prep time 15 min. Squash cook time 90 min.
Stock prep time 15 min. (while squash is cooking)
Total time - 2 hr.
Soup can be prepped, cooked and refrigerated up to 24 hr. ahead - reheat and assemble just prior to serving. Also freezes well
You will need a star-shaped or gingerbread man cookie cutter mold to make the "Wiggly Man"
You can use a sweet potato in place of a squash

Serves - 8 bowls

Four Squash Soup with a Wiggly Man
½ of each of 4 different types of squash - halved and seeded -
    leave skin on squash for baking
1 tsp. butter in each squash half
1 tsp. brown sugar in each squash half
2 large onions - peeled and chopped
2 Tbsp. butter

Four Squash Soup with a Wiggly Man...cont.
2 Tbsp. olive oil
2 C. sherry
3 C. chicken stock
2 C. heavy cream - you can use low fat cream or milk if you wish
1 C. sour cream cut with ¼ C. milk - mixed together
salt and pepper to taste

Four Squash Soup with a Wiggly Man
Squash
Preheat oven to 350°

Cover squash, butter, brown sugar with tinfoil and place on tray in oven
    cut side up, so melted sugar and butter stay in seed cavity

Bake until done - about 90 min.

Soup
In stock pot - sauté onions in 2 Tbsp. butter and 2 Tbsp. olive oil until
    golden

Add sherry and let simmer 10 min.

Add chicken stock

Remove squash from oven when done - (soft inside and cooked through)

Skin squash

Add squash and butter/sugar syrup from cooked squash to stock pot

Simmer 15 min.

Remove from heat and let cool

When cool - in batches purée in processor then pass through metal sieve

Prior to serving (45-30 min.) heat soup, add heavy cream and mix together

Plate
To serve - place star shaped (cookie cutter) mold in bottom of bowl

Fill star shaped mold with sour cream/milk mixture

Pour hot soup around star shaped mold

Remove star shaped mold gently lifting straight up

Four Squash Soup with a Sour Cream Wiggly Man

Potato Leek Soup (Hot and Cold, Green and White)

Time To Prepare and Tips
Prep time 15 min.
Cooking time 60 min. Cooling and Purée 30 min.
Assembly 15 min. Total time - 2 hr. 30 min.
Soup can be prepped, cooked and refrigerated up to 24 hr. ahead - just reheat leek soup and assemble just prior to serving

Serves - 8 bowls

Potato Soup	*Leek Soup*	*Garnish*
4 good size potatoes - peeled and cubed	4 leeks - cleaned, root end cut, use about 1" into the green - chopped	1 leek - cleaned, root end cut, use up to green - 3" julienne
2 Tbsp. butter	1 onion - peeled and chopped	1 C. vegetable oil (for frying leeks)
1 onion - peeled and chopped	2 Tbsp. butter	
½ C. vodka	2½ C. chicken stock	
2½ C. chicken stock	1 C. heavy cream	
1 C. heavy cream	green food color	
salt and white pepper to taste		

Potato Soup (served cold)
In pot - boil potatoes in water

In saucepan - sauté onion in 2 Tbsp. butter

Add vodka - cook down 5 min. - reserve mixture

When potatoes are soft - drain and add 2 C. chicken stock

Add sautéed onion/vodka mixture to potato/stock

Simmer potato/stock on low 15 min.

Allow to cool

Purée potato mixture, add 1 C. heavy cream,

Run through sieve

Place in bowl and set in ice bath, then refrigerate until pouring

Leek Soup (served hot)
In saucepan - sauté leeks and onion in 2 Tbsp. butter

Add 2 C. chicken stock and simmer on low 15 min.

Allow to cool

Purée mixture, add 1 C. heavy cream

Add tiny amount of green food color to obtain a good green color

Run through sieve

Leek Soup is served hot

Final Assembly
Place each color - green hot leek, white cold potato in separate pourable containers

At the same time - ***from opposite sides of the bowl*** - pour slowly from each container simultaneously

The bowl should fill with one half green and hot and the other half white and cold

Crispy Fried Leeks
Heat vegetable oil to very hot in large saucepan

Place the leeks (a handful at a time) in the very hot oil

Cover with splatter screen and allow to cook until slightly brown

Remove fried leeks with slotted spoon and place in paper towel lined bowl to de-grease

Continue until all leeks are crispy fried-set aside in paper towel lined bowl

Garnish
Crispy, fried leeks sprinkled on top of the soup

Cold Vodka Potato Soup and Hot Leek Soup with Crispy Fried leeks

Cold Strawberry Soup

Time To Prepare and Tips
Prep 5 min.
Cooking 20 min. Cooling and Puree 60 min.
Total time - 90 min.+-

Serves - 8 bowls

Cold Strawberry Soup
I - 10-12 oz. package frozen strawberries
3 C. orange juice
1 C. orange liqueur
1 C. heavy cream
2 C. plain yogurt

Garnish
1 large strawberry per serving - sliced and fanned

Cold Strawberry Soup
Bring frozen strawberries, orange juice and orange liqueur
    to boil

Lower heat and add heavy cream and yogurt

Bring back to boil

Remove from heat and allow to cool

When cool, purée in food processor

Cool in refrigerator

Plate
Serve cold in soup bowl

Garnish
Place sliced fanned strawberry on top of soup

Cold Strawberry Soup

Curried Squash and Pear Bisque - *Ruth and Ernst Luthi*

Time To Prepare and Tips
Prep 30 min.
Cooking 60 min.
Cooling and Purée time - 60 min.
Total time - 2 hr.+-

Serves - 8 bowls

Curried Squash and Pear Bisque
1 butternut squash - (About 2 lb.)
2 Tbsp. butter
2 C. Bartlett pears (about 1 lb.) - peeled, chopped
1½ C. onions - peeled and thinly sliced
1½ C. water
1 C. pear nectar - **not pear juice from a can of pears**
3 C. vegetable stock
1 C. pear liqueur

Curried Squash and Pear Bisque...cont.
4 tsp. curry powder
¼ tsp. salt
⅛ tsp. black pepper
½ C. half-and-half

Garnish
1 Bartlett pear - cored and thinly sliced

Curried Squash and Pear Bisque
Preheat oven to 375°

Cut squash in half lengthwise, discard seeds and membrane

Put squash halves cut side down on a baking-sheet, bake at 375° for
     45 min. or until tender

Remove squash from oven and cool

Peel squash, mash pulp - you will need 3½ C. of pulp for the soup

Melt butter in large Dutch oven

Add chopped pears, onion; sauté 10 min. or until lightly browned

Add squash pulp, water and next 6 ingredients

Bring to a boil, partly cover, reduce heat and simmer for 40 min.

Process squash mixture in blender until smooth

Return puréed mixture to pan and stir in half-and-half

Cook over low heat until thoroughly reheated

Plate
Serve hot in soup bowl

Garnish
Float pear slices on the bisque

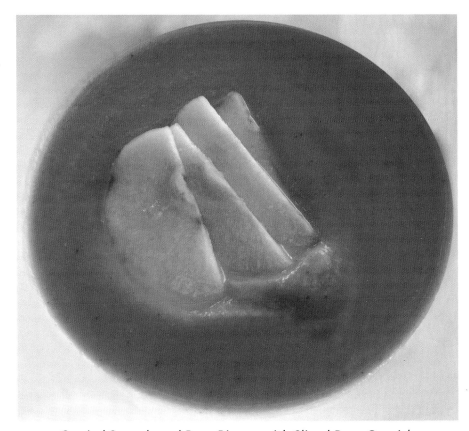

Curried Squash and Pear Bisque with Sliced Pear Garnish

Roasted Garlic and Brie

Time To Prepare and Tips
Prep 15 min   Marinate garlic heads minimum 20 min.
Bake garlic 40 min.
Assembly 5 min.
Total time - 1 hr.+-

Serves - 4

Garlic and Brie
4 garlic heads - cut top off garlic to expose top of cloves
½ C. olive oil
½ C. balsamic vinegar
½ - 8 oz. wheel Brie cheese - quartered - ¼ per serving

Garnish
24 miniature toasts, or gluten-free crackers+-
1 - 10-12 oz. can jumbo pitted black olives - chopped
2 ripe tomatoes - chopped
¼ C. capers
4 scallions - ends flared - see General Hints, Tips and Suggestions at
          beginning of book

Garlic and Brie
Place garlic heads in oven proof dish - exposed cloves up

Combine olive oil and balsamic vinegar and pour over garlic heads

Marinate garlic heads in oil mix - anywhere from 20 min. to 5 hr.

Drain off and reserve marinade

Place marinated garlic heads in oven proof dish

Preheat oven to 400°

Roast garlic heads in oven until cloves start to emerge from garlic
          heads - 30 min.+-

Remove garlic heads from oven and set aside

Add cheese wedges to oven dish and return to oven

Heat just until cheese starts to melt 2-5 min.+-

Plate
Prepare plates: toasts fanned, olives, tomatoes and capers spread
          around plates, scallion placed at top of plate

Place baked garlic heads on plate - exposed cloves up

Remove cheese from oven and put on plates close to garlic head

Garnish
Drizzle marinade over plate

Roasted Garlic Heads and Brie Cheese,
Olive Oil and Balsamic Vinegar with Capers, Diced Tomatoes,
and Gluten-Free Crackers

Grilled Squid

Time To Prepare and Tips
Prep 15 min.
Marinate minimum 1 hr.
Grill less than 15 min.
Assembly 5 min. Total time - 1 hr. 45 min .

Serves - 4

Grilled Squid
1 lb. squid - cleaned and sliced open - use cleaned heads as well
4 garlic cloves - peeled and minced
½ C. olive oil
½ C. dark rum
2 Tbsp. dried mint leaves - or a handful of fresh mint - chopped
salt and pepper to taste

Garnish
capers
diced tomatoes
diced black olives for garnish

Grilled Squid
Combine and marinate all squid ingredients for at least 1 hr. -
        (longer is OK)

Remove squid from marinade and grill until squid has curled
        NOT TOO LONG - 10-15 min.+-

Plate
Plate grilled squid centered on each plate

Garnish
Garnish with capers, tomatoes and olives over squid

Grilled Squid with Capers, Diced Olives and Diced Tomatoes

Pastry Wrapped Pork Tenderloin w/Chopped Spinach and Cheese

Time To Prepare and Tips

Prep 10 min.
Marinate minimum 30 min.
Bake 40 min.+-   Cool 10-15 min.
Assembly 5 min. Total time - 90 min.+-

Serves - 4

Pastry Wrapped Pork Tenderloin
1 small pork tenderloin
1 C. Mae Ploy Sweet Chili Sauce
4-6 oz. soft cheese (Gorgonzola, Brie, blue etc.)
1 - 10-12 oz. pack frozen chopped spinach - thawed and drained
1 pack Pepperidge Farm puff pastry - NOT phyllo- properly thawed

Garnish
½ C. warmed Mae Ploy Sweet Chili Sauce

Pastry Wrapped Pork Tenderloin

Preheat oven to 350°

Marinate pork in Mae Ploy Sweet Chili Sauce for at least 30 min.
      (longer is fine if refrigerated)

Mix cheese and prepared spinach together

Open pastry - use one sheet - return other sheet to freezer

Roll pastry out on floured cutting board

Place marinated pork tenderloin in center of pastry

Place cheese/spinach mixture on top of meat

Fold pastry over meat/cheese/spinach mixture - make sure it is totally enclosed

You will now have a tube of filled puff pastry

Place on a rack over an oven sheet

Bake for 40 min. or until pastry has puffed and browned

Remove from oven and when cooled - about 10 min. - cut into 1" slices

Plate
Place 2-3 slices centered on each plate

Garnish
Top pastry wrapped tenderloins with warm Mae Ploy Sweet Chili Sauce

Sweet Chili Sauce
Awesome on Everything!

Phyllo Purses w/Mushroom, Cheese and Cranberry

Time To Prepare and Tips
Prep 15 min.+-
Sauté 15-20 min.+-
Assembly 15 min.
Bake 20 min.+-
Total time - 1 hr.+-

Serves - 4

Phyllo Purses
½ lb. mushrooms - cleaned, stemmed and chopped very small
½ onion - peeled and chopped very small
1 shallot - peeled and chopped very small
½ tsp. thyme
1 Tbsp. olive oil

Phyllo Purses...cont.
1 package thawed phyllo pastry
½ lb. Brie cheese - room temperature - cut into 1" pieces
1 C. cranberries - blanched and cooled in cold water
2 Tbsp. balsamic vinegar
½ stick (2 oz.) butter - melted

Phyllo Purses
Preheat oven to 400°

Sauté - mushrooms, onion, shallots and thyme in olive oil - until
      mushrooms are cooked

Drain sautéed mixture and reserve

Lay out 1 sheet phyllo - paint entire sheet with butter

Repeat 4 times

Cut phyllo - lengthwise into thirds, then sideways into quarters

Place 1 tsp. mushroom mix into center of each phyllo square

Place small bit of Brie and 2 cranberries and 1 tsp. of balsamic
      vinegar into center of each phyllo square

Fold phyllo corners up and pinch together into a "purse"

Place on baking sheet and brush outside of purse with butter

Bake until golden brown - 10-20 min.

Can be made ahead and re-heated

Plate
Place 3 "purses" centered on each plate

Phyllo Purses with Mushroom, Cheese and Cranberry

Sweet Potato Nests of Shrimp

Time To Prepare and Tips
Prep 15 min.
Marinate 30 min. Sauté 5 - 7 min.
Fry sweet potatoes 15-20 min.
Reduce marinade into sauce 30 min.
Assembly 10 - 15 min. Total time - 2 hr.

Serves - 4

Shrimp Marinade
12 large raw shrimp - shelled, cleaned and deveined
2 Tbsp. black sesame seeds
1 tsp. curry
1 tsp. allspice
1 tsp. cayenne
1 C. dark rum
¼ C. brown sugar
½ C. sesame oil

Sweet Potato Nests
2 large sweet potatoes - peeled and shredded into long "shoestrings"
1½ C. oil - for frying sweet potatoes

soft lettuce OR mixed colored lettuce

Sweet Potato Nests of Shrimp
Marinate shrimp in marinade ingredients for 30 min. -
   remove shrimp and reserve marinade

Sauté shrimp and marinade on stove top until shrimp is just
   pink - 3-5 min.+-

Remove shrimp from sauce - set shrimp aside, keep marinade
   in pan

Reduce marinade to sauce consistency - 30 min.+-

Deep fry sweet potato strings in a small high sided pot - fry
   until crispy

Remove sweet potato strings and drain on paper towels

Plate
Place a bed of lettuce centered on each plate

Place a mound of sweet potatoes on lettuce and shape like
   a nest

Top each nest with 3 shrimp

Garnish
Drizzle warm sauce over each nest

Sweet Potato Nest of Shrimp
with Spicy Sauce on a Bed of Greens

Marinated Mushrooms on Polenta

Time To Prepare and Tips
Prep and marinade 30 min.
Sauté 15 - 20 min.
Cook down mushrooms 30 min.
Final cook down mushrooms 30 min.
Fry polenta 15 min.
Total time - 2 hr.+-.

Serves - 4

Marinated Mushrooms on Polenta
1 lb. mixed mushrooms - cleaned, stemmed and sliced thickly
1 C. cheap port
2 shallots - peeled and chopped
1 clove garlic - peeled and minced
1 Tbsp. butter

Marinated Mushrooms on Polenta...cont.
1 C. beef stock
½ C. heavy cream

1 store bought tube of polenta - sliced ¾" thick
1½ C. oil - for frying polenta

Marinated Mushrooms on Polenta
Marinate first 4 ingredients in ziploc bag - 15 min. - minimum

Sauté mushrooms, shallots, garlic and port in butter on
        medium to high - 30 min.

Add beef stock and reduce 20-30 min.

Remove mushrooms with slotted spoon and set aside

Add heavy cream to reducing stock and bring to boil

Reduce heat to medium for 10-15 min.

Add mushrooms to thickened sauce 15 min. prior to serving

Fry polenta slices in oil - turn over to fry both sides until crispy

Plate
Place a slice of fried/drained polenta centered on each plate

Using a slotted spoon - place mushrooms over polenta

Garnish
Spoon thickened sauce over mushrooms

Marinated Mushrooms on Polenta

Foie Gras (*the easiest, most impressive foodie thing you can do!*)

Time To Prepare and Tips

Toast pine nuts 5 min. Sear foie gras 5 min. Assembly 5 min.
Total time - 15 min.
The best source for single serving frozen foie gras is Amazon   no kidding!
You could also place the cooked foie gras on a bed of greens, or on a fried polenta round from the preceding page
This goes extremely well with Sauternes! It's my excuse for opening d'Yquem.

Serves - 4

Foie Gras
4 - 2 oz. frozen foie gras pieces
coarse salt

optional - bed of greens (any greens) or fried polenta round

Garnish
reduced balsamic vinegar - see General Hints, Tips and
　　　　　Suggestions at beginning of book
toasted pine nuts

Foie Gras
Top each piece of thawed foie gras with a couple pinches of
　　　　coarse salt **1 side only**

In a **very hot** and **dry pan** - place each piece of foie gras - salted
　　　　side down

After 2-3 min. - turn each piece over with spatula

After second side is cooked 2-3 min. - remove from pan with
　　　　spatula and place each piece on a plate

Reserve any melted foie gras in the pan and refrigerate for later
　　　　use (this makes an interesting fat)

Plate
Place each foie gras slice (salted side up) centered on each plate,
　　　　or on top of your bed of choice

Garnish
Squirt a squiggly line of reduced balsamic vinegar on the top of
　　　　the foie gras and over the plate

Sprinkle toasted pine nuts over top of the reduced balsamic

Seared Foie Gras with Reduced Balsamic Vinegar
and Toasted Pine Nuts

29

Gluten-Free Crab Cakes

Time To Prepare and Tips
Prep all ingredients 15 min.
Sauté onion, garlic, shallot 15 min. Mix all ingredients together 5 min.
Fry crab cakes 15 min. Plate 5 min.
Total time - less than 1 hr.
Crab cakes can be place directly on plate, or on a bed off greens, or any other bed of choice

Serves - 4 (2 cakes per)

Gluten-Free Crab Cakes (8 cakes)
1 onion - peeled and finely diced
4 garlic cloves - peeled and finely diced
1 shallot - peeled and finely diced
¼ C. olive oil (for sautéing ingredients)
¼ C. dark rum
2 - 8 oz. cans crab meat
1 red bell pepper - cleaned and finely diced

Gluten-Free Crab Cakes...cont.
2 C. gluten-free crackers - finely crushed
2 eggs
2 C. vegetable oil (for frying cakes)

Cocktail Sauce
1 C. ketchup
1+ Tbsp. horseradish - hotness to taste
½ tsp. lemon juice (to taste)

Gluten-Free Crab Cakes
Sauté onion, garlic, shallot and rum in olive oil

Add crab and continue cooking and stirring until heated through

Combine in large bowl - all sautéed items, raw red pepper dice,
      crushed crackers and 2 raw eggs

Mix well with your hands - make sure to incorporate everything

Make patties out of above mixture

Heat frying oil to very hot

Using metal spatula - slide crab patties into hot oil

Cook until brown and flip

Remove from hot oil and drain on paper towel

Cocktail Sauce
Combine all Cocktail sauce ingredients to taste

Plate
Place 2 crab cakes centered on each plate, or on bed of choice

Garnish
Place a dollop of cocktail sauce on top or on the side of
      crab cakes

Gluten-Free Crab Cake with Cocktail Sauce,
Red Pepper, and Cilantro Garnish

Pernod Mussels Over White Rice

Time To Prepare and Tips

Prep vegetables 15 min.
Cook rice 30 min. Cook mussels 5 min.
Ready to serve in 45 min. or less
I like the large frozen ½ shell green-lip mussels, but mussels "in the shell" are fine too
Make sure you have a "shell" plate or bowl for each person or the table

Serves - 4

Rice
2 C. chicken stock
2 Tbsp. butter
1 C. white rice

Garnish
sprigs of tarragon

Pernod Mussels
1 C. Pernod or Pastis other similar liqueur
1 C. vegetable stock
1 onion - peeled and diced fine
2 garlic cloves - peeled and diced fine
12 oz. diced tomatoes
2 lb. mussels

White Rice

Bring stock and butter to boil in covered saucepan

Add rice to boiling liquid, stir and cover

When water/rice boils again - reduce heat to low and cook covered for 20 min.

Keep warm until serving

Pernod Mussels

Combine all mussel ingredients except the mussels, together in a large, broad saucepan with cover

Allow to boil for 5 min.

When boiling, add mussels and continue boiling for 5-7 min.

If using mussels in the shell, do not use the mussels that do not open after boiling!

Plate

In a large bowl - place a scoop of cooked white rice

Spoon mussels and liquid into bowl over rice

Garnish

Sprinkle with tarragon

Pernod Mussels Over White Rice

Coconut Crusted Rack of Lamb w/Marsala Mint Sabayon, Sweet Potatoes and Lentils, and Sweet & Sour Red Cabbage

Time Line 3 hr.

Start 3 hr. before serving	45 min. after starting	1½ hr. after starting
Lamb 2 ½ hr.	prep (trim French) 30min. — make marinade 15 min.	marinate lamb 60 min. minimum
Sweet Potatoes 1½ hr.	clean, peel, cut sweet potatoes 15 min.	boil sweet potatoes 45 min.
Lentils 20 min.		parboil lentils 20 min.
Red Cabbage 1½ hr.		prep cabbage 15 min.
Mint Sabayon 1½ hr.	separate 4 eggs and reserve yolks	Mint Sabayon - cook mint sauce and Marsala wine 15 min.

Cooking Hints

The lamb can be prepped and frozen, or marinated and frozen until ready to grill and bake
All of these items can be made ahead of time and reheated as needed
Instead of mint jelly or sauce - try this Marsala mint sabayon (foam)
I strongly recommend adding a "whip-it" to your kitchen arsenal - instant real whipped cream!

A "Whip-it"
Whip Creamer

Serves - 4

Coconut Crusted Rack of Lamb
2 lamb racks - Frenched
1 C. shredded coconut
   Marinade (60 min. minimum)
2 garlic heads - peeled and minced
2 Tbsp. fresh ginger - skinned and chopped
2 C. red wine
2 C. black coffee
½ C. olive oil per rack
1 C. shredded coconut - toasted

Sweet & Sour Red Cabbage
½ head red cabbage - shredded
1 C. raspberry vinegar
½ C. white sugar, agave or other sweetener

Master Ingredient List

Sweet Potatoes and Lentils
4 large sweet potatoes
salt and pepper to taste
1 C. lentils
4 Tbsp. butter

Marsala Mint Sabayon
1 - 8-12 oz. jar mint jelly
1 C. Marsala wine
4 egg yolks

Garnish
fresh mint leaves

Wine Suggestions
2015 Mauvais Garcon (Bad Boy) - Thunevin
   - Bordeaux Blend $15
2013 Ferrer-Bobet Ferrer Bobet - Proprietary Blend $37
2014 Lagier Meredith - Syrah $45

Watch our "How to French a Rack of Lamb" video - www.boozehoundsguidetogourmet.com

Sweet Potatoes and Lentils

Peel and cut sweet potatoes to 1" cubes

Boil in salted and peppered water until soft 45 min.+-

Par-boil lentils in separate pot 20 min.+-

When sweet potatoes are soft - strain and mash

Add 1 Tbsp. butter per potato

Add semi-boiled lentils and fold in

Set aside warmed until ready to Plate

Sweet & Sour Red Cabbage

Clean (peel off outer layer) and shred red cabbage

Place shredded red cabbage in large covered sauce pan with raspberry vinegar and sweetener

Cover and cook for at least 30 min.
Uncover and continue to cook for another 30 min.

Sweet & Sour Red Cabbage...cont.

Make sure liquid does not cook out

Taste and if necessary - add more sweetener - you want the taste to be "sweet and sour" - not too much of either

Marsala Mint Sabayon

Combine 1 small jar of mint jelly with 1 C. Marsala wine

Bring to a boil and cook for 10 min.

Remove from heat and when cooled - whisk in 4 egg yolks and place mixture in refrigerator until ready Plate

Just before plating - put mixture in a whip-it

Use 2 - CO_2 cartridges for extra whipping

Test by foaming in sink prior to plating

When plating, put small dollop on top of each plated lamb chop

| 1½ hr. before serving | | 45 min. before serving | | Serve 3 hr. after starting |

| marinate lamb 60 min. minimum | grill/mark lamb - 5 min. then bake lamb 30 min.+- keep warm until serving |

| boil sweet potatoes 45 min. drain and mash | add butter and lentils to sweet potatoes - keep warm until serving |

| cook red cabbage 60 min. | keep warm until serving |

| Mint Sabayon - allow to cooled down 30 min. | Mint Sabayon - when cooled, whisk in egg yolks and whip to foam 15 min. |

Toasted Coconut

Place shredded coconut on sheet pan and place in 350° oven for 10-15 min. or until slightly toasted

When toasted remove from oven and place in large stainless bowl

Coconut Crusted Rack of Lamb

French each lamb rack (clean bones and cut away fat cap) marinate in puréed: garlic, red wine, coffee, olive oil and ginger

Watch how to French trim a rack of lamb on our website *www.boozehoundsguidetogourmet.com*

After a minimum of 60 min. - remove from marinade, pat dry and cut each rack in half

Preheat oven to 350°

Reserve marinade for future use - freeze in ziploc

Grill each side of rack on very hot grill until marked - 2-3 min./side

Place lamb pieces in 350° oven and cook to desired doneness - use an insta-read meat thermometer to check - rare 125°, medium 145°, well 160.

Remove from oven and cut rack halves into individual ribs

Roll finished lamb rack pieces in toasted coconut

Plate

Place 4 individual, coconut crusted lamb ribs, a serving of sweet potato lentils and a serving of sweet and sour red cabbage - each on ⅓ of each plate

Garnish

Apply Marsala mint sabayon foam on top of lamb ribs

Place mint sprigs on plate

Coconut Crusted Rack of Lamb with Marsala Mint Sabayon, Sambuca Oyster Mushroom Risotto (pg. 74) and Baked Cheesy Asparagus (pg.34)

Stuffed Pork Tenderloin w/Apricot Bacon Brandy Stuffing and Sauce, Saffron Risotto and Baked Cheesy Asparagus
(Ruth and Ernst Luthi)

Time Line 2 hr.

Start 2 hr. before serving	30 min. after starting	1 hr. after starting
Pork 1 hr.	trim fat, stuff and tie 20 min.	sear 3-5 min./side
Apricot Stuffing/Sauce 75 min. chop stuffing 10 min.	cook and purée stuffing 20 min.	
Risotto 30-40 min.	make saffron wine tea 30 min.	
Baked Asparagus 45 min.		

Cooking Hints

Pork, stuffing and asparagus can all be prepped well ahead and cooked just prior to serving
Risotto can be made ahead and only half cooked - last half cooking at the end

Serves - 4

Master Ingredient List

Pork Tenderloin
1 pork tenderloin
kitchen string or butcher elastic mesh
olive oil for browning

Apricot Bacon Brandy Stuffing
½ lb. bacon - finely diced
½ lb. dried apricots - finely diced
½ white onion - peeled and finely diced
1 shallot - peeled and finely diced
2 large garlic cloves- peeled and finely diced

Saffron Risotto
1 yellow or white onion - peeled and finely diced
½ C. olive oil
8 saffron threads
1 C. dry white wine
1 C. Arborio rice
2 C. stock (chicken or vegetable)
1 C. shredded or ground hard cheese

Baked Cheesy Asparagus
20 asparagus spears - cleaned and snapped
¼ C. truffle oil
1 C. grated cheese

Apricot Bacon Brandy Stuffing Sauce/Garnish
remainder of stuffing after filling pork tenderloins
½ C. brandy

Wine Suggestions
2013 Cherry Pie Cherry Tart - Chardonnay $15
2014 Lucia, Vineyards Santa Lucia Highlands
    - Chardonnay $39
2012 Chateau Montelena - Chardonnay $45

Apricot Bacon Brandy Stuffing

Sauté prepped: bacon, apricots, onion, shallot and garlic until bacon is cooked

Remove from pan, drain and lightly purée in blender

Set aside in bowl until ready to stuff pork

Baked Cheesy Asparagus

Preheat oven to 350°

Place prepped asparagus in a bowl - drizzle truffle oil over spears

Place oiled spears in a line or lines (all asparagus facing the same direction)

Sprinkle shredded cheese over asparagus

Place in preheated oven for 15 min.

Saffron Risotto

Preheat the stock

Sauté the onion in olive oil until cooked and starting to color

Place saffron in the white wine to make a saffron tea - remove saffron after 30 min. - reserve white wine/saffron tea

Add unrinsed Arborio rice to onions and mix in well - when almost dry, add white wine saffron tea and stir in well

Add half of the hot stock and stir well - cover and let sit on medium heat for 15 min. - reduce heat to low

30 min. prior to serving raise heat to medium high and add 2nd half of hot stock - stir into rice mixture and cover

Mix in cheese

Keep warm until serving

1 hr. before serving	30 min. before serving	Serve 2 hr. after starting

cook stuffed pork tenderloin 25 min. (longer for more doneness)

cook down remainder of stuffing and purée 45 min.

make risotto 45 min.

clean and cut asparagus 15 min.   bake asparagus 15 min.

Apricot Bacon Brandy Sauce

After stuffing pork, add leftover stuffing to ½ C. brandy and cook down, stirring constantly - allow brandy to flame off

Place stuffing/brandy mix in food processor and purée

Return purée to saucepan, and continue cooking puréed stuffing/brandy mix to sauce thickness

Stuffed Pork Tenderloin

Preheat oven to 425°

Clean pork tenderloin - remove fat and membrane

In a frying pan, sear tenderloin in hot oil, on all sides

Remove seared tenderloin

Slice seared tenderloin halfway through along the length (like a hot dog bun)

Fill the cut with cooked bacon/apricot stuffing - maybe ¾" thick

Tie and bind cut, stuffed, tenderloin with kitchen string, or place inside butcher elastic mesh

Place stuffed, bound pork tenderloin on rack in baking dish

Bake at 425° for 20-25 min. or until an insta-read meat thermometer reads at least 145°

Keep warm until ready to serve

Remove binding and slice cooked pork into ¾" thick medallions

Plate

Place a serving of risotto centered on each plate

Fan 3 medallions of pork on one side of risotto

Place a serving of asparagus spears across the other side of the risotto

Garnish

Spoon stuffing sauce over pork medallions

Pork Tenderloin with Apricot Bacon Brandy Stuffing and Sauce,
Garlic Sage Roasted Fingerling Potatoes (pg. 58)
Brussels Sprout Fluff (pg. 48) and
Sambuca Tarragon Cherry Tomatoes (pg. 42),

35

Jimmy's Cinnamon Red Chili Beef Tenderloin Steaks w/Green Chili Hollandaise, Port Mushrooms,
(Jimmy McGuinness)   Baked Sweet Potato Fries and Garlic Broccoli

Time Line 2 hr.

Start 2 hr. before serving	30 min. after starting	1 hr. after starting
Beef 45 min.	trim fat, cut into steaks 15 min.	marinate 15 min. minimum
Green Chili Hollandaise 45 min.		boil green chili hollandaise 15 min.
Mushrooms 1¼ hr.	clean, slice mushrooms 15 min.	marinate mushrooms 15 min. minimum
Sweet Potato Fries 1¼ hr.		peel and cut sweet potato fries 30 min.
Garlic Broccoli 45 min.		

Cooking Hints

Steaks can be prepped and marinated ahead - it's even OK to freeze - marinated or not - for later in packs of 2 or 4
Keep unused Hollandaise for in the refrigerator - use it on anything - great on eggs at breakfast - lasts for a long time refrigerated
Any left over cinnamon chili mix can be frozen for later use

Serves - 4

Cinnamon Red Chili Tenderloin Steaks
1 beef tenderloin - trimmed and cut to 2" steaks
½ C. olive oil
¼ C. cinnamon
¼ C. red chili - hot and spicy is good!

Green Chili Hollandaise Sauce
¼ C. butter or non-dairy butter or olive oil
2 heaping Tbsp. Knorr Hollandaise powder
2 - 14 oz. cans coconut milk - shaken prior to opening
1 - 13 oz. tub New Mexico green chili - hot is best

Master Ingredient List

Port Mushrooms
1 lb. mushrooms - cleaned, stemmed, sliced
   (I use crimini, but anything will work)
1 C. cheap port - I use jug tawny
1 C. stock reduced to thick syrup consistency
   (any stock is fine - beef, chicken, veg.)

Baked Sweet Potato Fries
2 large sweet potatoes
¼ C. olive oil
salt and pepper to taste

Garlic Broccoli
1 head broccoli cleaned down to florets and
   cleaned and cut stems
4 garlic cloves - peeled and sliced
¼ C. sesame oil
¼ C. olive oil

Wine Suggestions
2014 Columbia Crest Grand Estates
   - Cab Sauvignon $10
2015 Prisoner Wine Co. Saldo - Zinfandel $24
2014 Lagier Meredith - Syrah $45

Green Chili Hollandaise Sauce

Melt or heat fat of your choice in large saucepan

When fat is hot, add Hollandaise powder and blend well

Add coconut milk to fat/Hollandaise mix - stir well

Add green chili

Boil for 15 min. then simmer for 30 min.

Heat prior to using - refrigerate unused sauce in sealed container

Port Mushrooms

Marinate sliced mushrooms in port for at least 30 min.

Add mushrooms and port to sauce pan with reduced stock

Cook in covered saucepan for 30 min.+ - make sure mushrooms do
   not cook dry - if they start to - add more port

Remove lid and continue to cook until liquid is thick and almost gone

Keep warm until serving

Baked Sweet Potato Fries

Preheat oven to 350°

Clean, peel and cut into "French fry" shape - thick or thin fries
   - your choice

Toss fries in olive oil and place on baking sheet - single layer thick

Salt and pepper to taste

Bake for 45 min. - more or less based on desired crispiness and size
   and thickness of cut

Garlic Broccoli

Add prepped broccoli, garlic and sesame oil to boiling water

Boil for 15 min. - drain and set aside

Prior to serving - stir fry in olive oil 5-10 min.

...continued

1 hr. before serving	30 min. before serving	Serve 2 hr. after starting

grill steaks 15 min. maximum

simmer green chili hollandaise 30 min. - keep warm until serving

cook mushrooms 45 min.

bake sweet potato fries 45 min.

clean and trim garlic/broccoli 15 min.	steam garlic/broccoli 15 min.	stir fry garlic/broccoli 5-10 min.

Beef Tenderloin Steaks

Preheat grill to very hot 30 min. prior to grilling

Cut tenderloin into 2" thick steaks

Reserve any trim or small pieces for later use - freeze trim in labeled ziploc bag

Rub steaks in olive oil

Rub oiled steaks in cinnamon-chili powder

Marinate at least 15 min.

Put rubbed steaks on hot grill - start with 3 min. per side...

Use an insta-read meat thermometer to check - rare 125°, medium 145°, well 160°

Plate

Place a serving of mushrooms on ⅓ of each plate

Top mushrooms with a steak

Place a serving of sweet potato fries on ⅓ of plate

Place a serving of vegetables on ⅓ of plate

Garnish

Drizzle green chili hollandaise over cooked steak

Jimmy's Cinnamon Red Chili Tenderloin, Port Mushrooms, Green Chili Hollandaise, Sweet Potato Fries, Grilled Sesame Brussels Sprouts and Truffled Corn (pg. 76) and Arugula Salad, w/Toasted Pine Nuts, Craisins, Chevre (pg. 7)

Veal Osso Buco w/Crispy Fried Leeks, Polenta and Roasted Root Vegetables

Time Line 4 hr.

Start 4 hr. before serving		1 hr. after starting	2 hr. after starting
Veal 4 hr. min.	prep(trim fat) 10 min.	sear 3 min./side	cook veal 4 hr. minimum
Roasted Root Vegetables 1 ¼ hr.		clean and cut vegetables 15 min.	
Polenta 30 min.			
Garnish - fried leeks 30 min.			

Cooking Hints

It's OK to cook the veal longer, or even ahead of time and keep warmed until serving
Veal dredging flour can be gluten-free
You can change stock to vegetable or chicken
Butcher elastic mesh is very useful in keeping food items together that have a tendency to come apart during cooking

Serves - 4

Veal
4 veal shanks (Osso Buco)
kitchen string or butcher elastic mesh
1 C. flour for dredging (you can also add red chili
     powder to the flour)
¾ C. olive oil
2 onions - peeled and diced
1 head garlic - peeled and minced
2 shallots - peeled and diced
3 C. stock - beef or veal (keep boiling until used)
1 C. port (keep boiling until used)
1 - 14 oz. can diced tomatoes (drained)

keep in mind - you want enough liquid to cover veal
shanks when baking, so adjust stock and port quantity
to number of shanks and baking container size

Master Ingredient List

Roasted Root Vegetables
2 large carrots - peeled, thick julienne
1 head garlic (down to peeled cloves)
2 shallots (down to cleaned segments)
1 butternut squash - peeled and cubed 1"
2 parsnips - peeled and thick julienne
¼ C. olive oil

Polenta
1 C. raw polenta (corn meal)
2 C. stock (chicken or vegetable)
1 Tbsp. butter
1 C. shredded or ground hard cheese
salt and pepper to taste

Garnish
1 leek - cleaned, root end cut, use up to green,
    - 3" julienne
1 C. vegetable oil (for frying leeks)

Wine Suggestions
2013 Luna Vineyards Lunatic Red -
    Proprietary Blend $9
2012 Fontanafredda Barolo Serralunga -
    Nebbiolo $27
2013 Conterno, Aldo Barolo - Nebbiolo $59

Polenta
Place 2 C. stock (chicken or vegetable) in saucepan

Add butter

Add 1 C. raw polenta

Cover and cook until polenta is done - 20 min.+-

Add cheese and mix

Keep warm until serving

Roasted Root Vegetables
Preheat oven to 350°

Combine carrots, garlic, shallots, squash and parsnips in large bowl

Add olive oil and toss

Roasted Root Vegetables...cont.
Place oiled root vegetables in tinfoil covered baking dish and roast
    for at least 1 hr. (open oven and shake or stir every 20 min.)
Remove tinfoil for last 15 min. of roasting

Crispy Fried Leeks
Heat vegetable oil to very hot in large saucepan

Place a handful at a time of the leeks in the hot oil

Cover with splatter screen and allow to cook until slightly brown

Remove fried leeks with slotted spoon and place in paper towel
    lined bowl to de-grease

Continue until all leeks are crispy fried

...continued

2 hr. before serving		1 hr. before serving		Serve 4 hr. after starting

cook veal 4 hr. minimum

roast vegetables at least 1 hr. - keep warm until serving

cook polenta 30 min.

julienne leeks 15 min.

fry leeks 15 min.

Veal Osso Buco

Preheat oven to 350°

Remove fat and silver from perimeter of each veal shank and bind with string or butcher elastic mesh

Heat olive oil in heavy pan

Toss prepped veal shanks in olive oil, dredge in flour, then sear both sides in hot oil in heavy pan 3-5 min. per side

Tightly pack seared veal in an oven proof heavy pan with cover

Keep oil in first heavy pan for vegetables

Sauté onion, garlic and shallots in oil - remove and set aside when cooked

Cover veal shanks with sautéed vegetables, boiling stock and port

Place covered veal, vegetables and liquid in oven for 2½ hr.

After 2½ hr. add can of drained diced tomatoes to top of veal mixture

Re-cover and cook for at least another 1½ hr.

Plate

Remove veal from heavy pan with slotted spoon and remove string or butcher elastic mesh

Place veal atop a scoop of polenta in the center of each plate

Spoon roasted root vegetables around the polenta/veal pile

Garnish

Spoon liquid from veal baking dish on top of veal

Top veal with a handful of crispy leeks

Osso Buco with Crispy Fried Leeks, Polenta and Roasted Root Vegetables

Balsamic Braised Short Ribs *(Seattle Times)* w/Mary's Onion Soup Potatoes and Truffle Steamed Green Beans

Time Line 3 hr.

Start 3 hr. before serving	45 min. after starting	1½ hr. after starting
Short Ribs over 2 days - 3-4 hr.	sear ribs 15 min. brown short rib vegetables 15 min.	cook remaining of rib ingredients 4-5 hr.
Roasted Potatoes 1hr.+-		
Steamed Beans 45 min.		

Cooking Hints

This is best if the ribs are started the day before and finished during the 3 hr. prior to serving - these instructions follow this method
You can use fingerling potatoes instead of cutting up larger potatoes

Serves - 4

Master Ingredient List

Balsamic Braised Short Ribs
1 Tbsp. vegetable or canola oil
8 bone-in short ribs (about 3 lb.)
2 leeks - cleaned, root end cut, white
    parts only, sliced
2 yellow onions - peeled and sliced
2 carrots, peeled and cut into 1" pieces
2 stalks celery, cut into 1" pieces
4 garlic cloves - peeled and chopped
1 tsp. red pepper flakes
1 tsp. salt
½ tsp. ground black pepper
2 Tbsp. tomato paste

Balsamic Braised Short Ribs...cont.
1 Tbsp. Dijon mustard
3 sprigs fresh rosemary
3 C. balsamic vinegar
¼ C. packed brown sugar
4 C. unsalted beef stock
3 C. red wine

Mary's Onion Soup Potatoes
4 potatoes - cleaned but not peeled, cut into 1"chunks
1 Tbsp. olive oil
1 package Lipton onion soup mix - (can be
    marinated for up to 5 hr.)

Truffle Steamed Green Beans
1 lb. green beans - snipped and prepped
1 Tbsp. truffle oil
water to cover beans

Wine Suggestions
2006 Chateau les Grand Chenes
    - Bordeaux Blend $20
2014 Round Pond Rutherford Estate
    - Cabernet Sauvignon $38
2011 Silver Oak - Cabernet Sauvignon $110

Mary's Onion Soup Potatoes
Parboil cut up prepped potatoes - should take about 10 min.

Preheat oven to 350°

Drain potatoes and place in bowl with olive oil and onion soup mix

Frequently toss potato ingredients

Empty potato ingredients into oven baking pan and cover with foil

Place in oven and bake until potatoes are done (45 min.+-) stirring a
    couple times through baking process

Truffle Steamed Green Beans
Place prepped beans in saucepan with cover

Add water to cover beans

Add truffle oil

Bring to a boil and steam - 10-15 min.

Keep warm until serving

Balsamic Braised Short Ribs (day before)
Preheat oven to 325°

In a large, heavy-bottomed pot, heat the oil over medium heat

Sear the short ribs for 3-4 min. on each side, or until well browned

Transfer the short ribs to a plate

Add the leeks, onions, carrots, celery and garlic to the pot and cook
    until well browned, stirring occasionally, about 12-15 min.

Add red pepper flakes, salt, pepper and tomato paste and cook until
    the tomato paste turns brick reddish-brown color, 6-7 min.

Add the Dijon mustard, rosemary sprigs, 1½ C. of balsamic vinegar
    and brown sugar

Scrape up any browned bits from the bottom of the pot

Return the short ribs to the pot, then add 2 C. beef stock and
    1½ C. red wine

1¼ hr. before serving		45 min. before serving		Serve 3 hr. after starting

cook rib ingredients 1 - 5 hr. · reduce cooking liquid - 30 min. at end				
clean, cut potatoes 10 min.	parboil potatoes 10-15 min.		mix potato ingredients and roast potatoes 45 min. total	
	prep beans 15 min.		Steam green beans 10-15 min.	

Balsamic Braised Short Ribs (day before)...cont.

Bring the mixture up to a low simmer and cover

The pot can be left on the stove top on low heat or placed in a 325° oven for 2-2½ hr.

Remove ribs and vegetables from liquid and refrigerate ribs and vegetables (together) as well as the liquid in pot overnight

Balsamic Braised Short Ribs (day of serving)

On the day of serving - take ribs/vegetables and liquid from refrigerator, remove solidified fat from top of liquid

Add ribs/vegetables back to (fat removed) liquid

Add 2 C. beef stock, 1½ C. balsamic vinegar and 1½ C. of wine to pot

Place in oven at 325° and continue cooking for 2-3 hr.

When done cooking, carefully transfer the meat to a platter

Cover with tinfoil and a couple kitchen towels to keep warm

Using a slotted spoon, remove and discard the solids from the liquid

Bring the liquid to a boil on the stove top and cook until reduced to 1 C.

Return ribs to reduced liquid and coat

Plate

Place a serving of short ribs, potatoes and green beans - each on ⅓ of each plate

Balsamic Braised Short Ribs with Mary's Onion Soup Potatoes and Truffle Steamed Green Beans

Elk Tenderloin w/Gin Juniper Sauce, Chipotle Coconut Scalloped Sweet Potatoes and Sambuca Tarragon Cherry Tomatoes

Time Line 2 hr.

Start 2 hr. before serving	30 min. after starting	1 hr. after starting
Elk Tenderloin 2 hr.	clean elk 15 min.	marinate elk 1 hr.
Scalloped Potatoes 2 hr.	boil coconut milk/chipotle mixture 20 min.	clean, peel and slice sweet potatoes 15 min.
Sambuca Tomatoes 1 hr.		
Elk marinade into sauce 30 min.		

Cooking Hints

The elk can be prepped and frozen, or marinated and frozen until ready to grill or bake
The scalloped sweet potatoes can be made ahead of time and reheated as needed - use a round circle cutter for a clean cut when serving
Cook the tomatoes at the last minute - leftover tomatoes are great on eggs the next day!

Serves - 4

Master Ingredient List

Elk
2 elk tenderloins - 1½-2 lb. total
Marinade (60 min. minimum)
½ C. olive oil
2 garlic cloves - peeled and minced
½ C. gin
¼ C. juniper berries - crushed
¼ C. dried thyme

Chipotle Coconut Scalloped Sweet Potatoes
4 large sweet potatoes
3 - 14 oz. cans coconut milk
2 - 7 oz. cans chipotle peppers

Sambuca Tarragon Cherry Tomatoes
2 small packs cherry tomatoes - use 8-10 per person
    - OK to mix color
1 C. Sambuca
½ C. fresh tarragon (dried will do in a pinch, but use less)

Wine Suggestions
2010 Bernardus - Pinot Noir SLH $16
2014 Drouhin, Domaine Willamette Valley
    - Pinot Noir $31
2013 Rossignol Trapet, Domaine Gevrey Chambertin
    Vieilles Vignes - Pinot Noir $45

Chipotle Coconut Scalloped Sweet Potatoes

Preheat oven to 350°

Wash, peel and slice (¼") the sweet potatoes

In a pot, combine coconut milk and chipotle peppers - boil 20 min.

Strain boiled mixture and discard chipotle pepper residue

In a 2" deep oven dish - place a layer of the sliced sweet potatoes

Ladle the coconut chipotle pepper mixture over sweet potatoes

Place another layer of sliced sweet potatoes

Ladle the coconut chipotle pepper mixture over sweet potatoes

Continue layering sweet potatoes and chipotle pepper mixture until done

Cover with tinfoil and bake for 60 min.

Chipotle Coconut Scalloped Sweet Potatoes...cont.

When baked, leave covered to set (can be frozen or refrigerated) and reheated

Drain off excess chipotle pepper liquid from baking dish prior to serving

Sambuca Tarragon Cherry Tomatoes

Rinse tomatoes and drain

Place tomatoes in a large bowl with Sambuca and tarragon

Marinate for 15 min. minimum (up to 1 hr. is fine)

Place tomatoes, Sambuca and tarragon in large saucepan w/cover

Cook on high for 5-10 min. allowing the alcohol to burn off

Keep covered and cook for another 5-10 min. - careful not to over cook tomatoes

...continued

1 hr. before serving		30 min. before serving	Serve 2 hr. after starting
marinate elk 1 hr		grill or bake elk 15-30 min	
bake scalloped sweet potatoes 60 min.			
clean and marinate tomatoes 30 min.		cook tomatoes 15-25 min.	
		cook down elk marinade to sauce 30 min.	

Elk Tenderloin

Clean and trim elk - remove fat and silver membrane

Marinate elk in all marinade ingredients for at least 1 hr. - can be marinated for 1 hr. or frozen in the marinade for future use

Preheat oven to 475° or start grill

Remove elk from marinade and either grill or bake

If grilling - place on hot grill until done to desired temperature

If baking - place on a rack over a baking sheet at 475° for 10-15 min. then reduce temperature to 300° until desired doneness

Use an insta-read meat thermometer to check - rare 125°, medium 145°, well 160°

When elk is cooked - let it sit out of heat for 10-15 min.

Slice into 1" thick medallions

Gin Juniper Sauce

Strain juniper berries out of marinade

Place marinade into saucepan and reduce to thick sauce consistency - 30 min.+-

Purée and reheat for serving

Plate

Place 2 or 3 sliced elk medallions on ⅓ of each plate

Place a serving of chipotle coconut scalloped sweet potatoes on ⅓ of plate

Place a serving of Sambuca tarragon cherry tomatoes on ⅓ of plate

Garnish

Sprinkle plate with juniper berries and/or tarragon

Spoon thickened sauce over elk

Elk Tenderloin with a Gin Juniper Sauce, Chipotle Coconut Scalloped Sweet Potatoes and Sambuca Tarragon Cherry Tomatoes

Pork Tenderloin w/Soy Maple Brandy Sauce, Sambuca Oyster Mushroom Quinoa and Eggplant Timbales

Time Line 2 hr.

Start 2 hr. before serving	30 min. after starting	1 hr. after starting
Pork 2 hr. min.	prep(trim fat) 10 min.	make marinade 5 min.	marinate pork 30 min.++

Soy Maple Marinade 35 min.

Quinoa 30-40 min.

Oyster Mushrooms 1 hr. — clean slice and marinate oyster mushrooms 30 min.

Eggplant Timbales 90 min.+- — prep, clean and bake eggplant 45-60 min.

Cooking Hints

All of these menu items can be made hours ahead and reheated
The pork can be prepped and marinated ahead or even frozen in the marinade and then thawed and cooked an hour ahead of dinner

Serves - 4

Master Ingredient List

Pork Tenderloin
1 lb. pork tenderloin
  Marinade (30 min. minimum)
¾ C. soy sauce (OK to use low sodium, or gluten-free)
1 C. maple syrup
  (OK to use alternate - agave etc.)
½ C. brandy - **sauce only, not marinade**

Sambuca Oyster Mushrooms
1 lb. oyster mushrooms - cleaned and cut large dice - 1" pieces
1 C. Sambuca

Quinoa
1 C. colored or rainbow quinoa
2 C. stock (chicken or vegetable is best)
1 Tbsp. oil or butter (any flavored oil could work

Eggplant Timbales
4 custard cups - buttered

1 large eggplant - baked - 45 min. - 375°, cooled, skinned, seeded
1 C. milk
¾ C. heavy cream
4 whole eggs

Eggplant Timbales...cont.
1 egg whites
1 tsp. sage
salt and pepper to taste

Garnish
sage sprigs or dried sage

Wine Suggestions
2012 Eubea Aglianico del Vulture Covo dei Briganti $18
2011 Schieferkopf (Chapoutier) Riesling Lieu-Dit Buehl $27
2014 Gruaud Larose - Bordeaux Blend $52

Sambuca Oyster Mushrooms

In a large bowl combine cut mushrooms and Sambuca

Marinate for at least 30 min.

In a large saucepan (with a lid):

Bring mushroom Sambuca to boil and cook covered for 15 min.

Uncover and cook until almost dry (add more Sambuca if mushrooms cook dry)

Set cooked mushrooms aside to add to cooked quinoa

Quinoa

In a 2 qt. (at least) pot with cover - add:
1 C. quinoa, 2 C. stock and oil or butter

Cover and bring to boil

Reduce heat to simmer until cooked

Add cooked mushrooms and keep warm - covered

Eggplant Timbales

Preheat oven to 350°

Combine all Eggplant Timbales ingredients and mix well with electric beaters

Fill buttered custard cup with eggplant mixture

Place filled custard cup in bain (water bath) and place in oven

Reduce temperature to 300°

Bake until firmly set - about 60 min

To serve cut around the perimeter of the cup with a knife and then unmold custard and plate upside down

Pork Tenderloin

Marinate pork for at least 30 min.

Preheat oven to 350°

Remove pork from marinade

1 hr. before serving	10 min. before serving	Serve 1 hr. after starting

cook pork 40-60 min.

cook down marinade 30 min.   keep warm until serving

make quinoa 30 min.+-

sauté oyster mushrooms 30 min.

bake timbales 40 min.

Pork Tenderloin...cont.

Place marinated pork in baking dish

Place in 350° oven, uncovered, for at least 40 min. (longer for more doneness)

Use an insta-read meat thermometer - pork should be 145°

When cooked to desired doneness - remove from heat and let sit for 10 min.

Slice into ½" thick medallions

Soy Maple Brandy Sauce

When pork has bean removed from soy maple marinade place marinade and ½ C. brandy in pot and bring to boil

Continue to cook down and reduce to sauce consistency - as sauce thickens, taste - add soy or maple as necessary

When desired sauce thickness is achieved turn off heat

Reheat prior to serving

Plate

Place 2 or 3 pork medallions, 1 eggplant timbale and a serving of Sambuca mushroom quinoa - each on ⅓ of each plate

Garnish

Drizzle soy maple brandy sauce over pork medallions

Garnish with sage sprig or sprinkle dried sage over plate

Pork Tenderloin with Soy Maple Brandy Sauce, Sambuca Oyster Mushroom Quinoa and Eggplant Timbale

Meatloaf w/Port Mushrooms, Asiago Mashed Potatoes and Truffle Baked Green Beans

Time Line 2 hr.

Start 2 hr. before serving		30 min. after starting		1 hr. after starting
Meatloaf 1½ hr.	clean and prep all 15 min.	sauté all vegetables 15 min.	mix all meatloaf ingredients 5 min.	
Mushrooms 1¼ hr.	clean, slice, marinate mushrooms 30 min.		cook mushrooms 45 min.	
Meatloaf Topping 40 min.	clean and prep all 15 min.	sauté all vegetables 20 min.	purée all topping ingredients 5 min.	
Mashed Potatoes 1 hr..	peel, cut potatoes 15 min.	boil potatoes 30 min.		
Green Beans 30 min.		prep and marinate green beans 15 min.		

Cooking Hints

This freezes well
Try interesting different ground meats - even ground poultry
If the topping is too sweet, add more Key Lime juice

Serves - 4

Master Ingredient List

Meatloaf
½ lb. ground bison
½ lb. ground lamb
½ lb. ground veal
1 C. gluten-free crackers - crushed
3 eggs
1 onion - peeled and finely diced
5 garlic cloves - peeled and finely diced
1 shallot - peeled and finely diced
½ C. dark rum
1 large carrot - peeled and finely diced
½ C. olive oil for above vegetables
olive oil or butter to grease baking
    loaf pan

Meatloaf Topping
6 oz. dried apricots - diced
2 garlic cloves - peeled and minced
½ lb. bacon cut to ½" pieces
1 Tbsp. olive oil
½ - 14 oz. can mandarin oranges - drained
½ C. brandy
1 Tbsp. Key Lime juice

Port Mushrooms
½ lb. mushrooms - cleaned, stemmed, sliced
1 C. beef stock reduced to thick syrup
    consistency
1 C. cheap port - I use jug tawny

Asiago Mashed Potatoes
4 large potatoes - peeled, cut into 1" chunks
1 C. shredded Asiago cheese
¼ lb. butter

Green Beans
1 lb. fresh green beans - ends snipped
¼ C. Truffle oil

Wine Suggestions
Chianti
2013 Ferrari-Carano - Merlot $15
2013 Foley Johnson Rutherford
        - Cabernet Sauvignon $29
2012 Paloma - Merlot $57

Port Mushrooms

Marinate prepped and sliced mushrooms in port for at least 30 min.

Add mushrooms and port to sauce pan with reduced stock

Cook in covered saucepan for at least 30 min. - make sure does not cook dry - if it does add more port

Remove lid and continue to cook until liquid is thick and almost gone - 15-20 min.

Asiago Mashed Potatoes

Boil prepped potatoes in large covered pot for 30 min.

Strain and mash adding butter during mashing

Asiago Mashed Potatoes...cont.

Add Asiago cheese and butter to mashed potatoes

Mix potatoes/cheese/butter

Keep warm until serving

Truffle Baked Green Beans

Preheat oven to 350°

Toss cleaned and trimmed green beans in Truffle oil

Spread out on baking sheet - single bean height

Place in oven 15-20 min.

Reduce heat and keep warm until serving

1 hr. before serving		30 min. before serving		Serve 2 hr. after starting

cook meatloaf 1 hr.

cook mushrooms 45 min.

mash potatoes 15 min.

bake green beans 15 min.

Meatloaf Topping

Heat 2 Tbsp. olive oil in saucepan

Sauté all Meatloaf Topping ingredients except Brandy and Key Lime juice

When sautéed, add Brandy and allow to burn off

Purée and add Key Lime juice - continue to purée until smooth

Meatloaf

Preheat oven 350°

Combine all ground meat in large bowl - set aside

Sauté onion, shallot garlic, carrots and dark rum - 15 min.

Add above sautéed ingredients, crushed crackers, cooked mushrooms, and eggs to mixed ground meat - mix well with hands

Place mixture in oiled or buttered loaf pan

Top mixture in loaf pan with "Meatloaf Topping"

Place in oven for 60 min.

When done, remove from heat and let rest 15 min. before serving

Plate

Slice layers from loaf pan

Place a sliced layer of meatloaf onto ⅓ of each plate

Place a serving of Asiago mashed potato onto ⅓ of plate

Place a serving of truffle baked green beans onto ⅓ of plate

Gluten-Free, Bison, Lamb, Veal Meatloaf with Baked Sweet Potato Fries (pg. 36) and Baked Cheesy Asparagus (pg. 34)

Herbed Veal Chops w/Mashed Cauliflower, Brussels Sprout Fluff and Burnt Cherry Rum Shishito Peppers

Time Line 1 hr.

Start 1 hr. before serving		15 min. after starting	½ hr. after starting
Veal Chops 45 min.	trim fat and silver 15 min.	marinate in oil 15 min. minimum	
Mashed Cauliflower 45 min.		trim cauliflower 10 min.	boil and mash cauliflower 30 min.
Brussels Sprout fluff 1 hr.	clean, slice and fluff 15 min.	marinate fluff 15 min. minimum	
Cherry Rum Peppers 1 hr.	clean, and dice peppers 15 min.	marinate peppers in cherry rum 15 min. minimum	

Cooking Hints

Typically - 1 thick chop per serving
Chops can be prepped and marinated ahead refrigerated - it's even OK to freeze for later in packs of 2 or 4
You can start to accumulate "fluff" whenever you clean Brussels sprouts - keep a ziploc bag in the fridge and add to it

Serves - 4

Master Ingredient List

Herbed Veal Chops
4 veal chops - trimmed and silvered
 Marinade (15 min. minimum)
½ C. olive oil
½ C. each of fresh: tarragon, rosemary, oregano
 leaves pulled off stems
½ C. Madeira

Brussels Sprout Fluff
1 lb. Brussels sprouts - cleaned, stemmed and
 broken down to individual leaf layers

Brussels Sprout Fluff...cont.
¼ C. sesame oil
salt and pepper to taste

Burnt Cherry Rum Sweet Peppers
1 C. Bacardi Burnt Cherry Rum plus 2 shot glasses
10 sweet shishito peppers - cleaned and diced
4 sweet colored peppers - cleaned and diced
2 Tbsp. olive oil
6 garlic cloves - peeled and minced
1 large shallot - peeled and finely diced

Mashed Cauliflower
2 heads cauliflower
1 C. grated or shredded hard cheese -
 (Parm, Romano, Asiago)
½ C. butter, oil, or other fat (foie gras drippings?)
salt and pepper to taste

Additional fresh herbs for garnish

Wine Suggestions
2014 Landmark Overloook - Pinot Noir $17
2011 Macphail Sundawg Ridge - Pinot Noir $32
2014 Hilt Vanguard - Pinot Noir $50

Mashed Cauliflower

Wash and clean cauliflower, removing thick stems and leaves

Break down to florets

Boil florets in water or stock mixture until mashable (45 min.)

Drain boiled cauliflower and mash

Add butter, oil or other fat and cheese and mix well

Salt and pepper to taste

Keep warm until serving

Brussels Sprout Fluff

Preheat oven to 350°

Mix Brussels sprout fluff with sesame oil and salt and pepper

Brussels Sprout Fluff...cont.

Marinate in sesame oil for at least 15 min.

Spread fluff on baking sheet

Bake for 30 min.

Reduce heat and keep warm until combining with Shishito peppers

Burnt Cherry Rum Shishito Peppers

Marinate all diced peppers in burnt cherry rum for 15 min.

Sauté garlic and shallots

Add rum marinated peppers and burn off alcohol

When mix is dry, add a shot glass of burnt cherry rum and burn off

When mix is dry, add second shot glass of the rum and burn off

Set aside and combine with Brussels sprout fluff to serve

...continued

¼ hr. before serving		15 min. before serving		Serve 1 hr. after starting
			grill chops 15 min. maximum	
	boil and mash cauliflower 30 min.			
	bake fluff 30 min.			
	sauté peppers 30 min.			

Herbed Veal Chops

Marinate veal in oil and fresh herbs and Madeira

Marinate at least 15 min.

Preheat grill to very hot 30 min. prior to grilling

Remove from marinade and top chops on grill with half of herb/oil/Madeira mixture

Add remaining herb/oil/Madeira mix to flipped side of chop

Grill to desired doneness - medium - about 4-5 min. per side use an insta-read meat thermometer to check - rare 125°, medium 145°, well 160°

Garnish

Place fresh herbs on top of veal chop

Plate

Place 1 herbed veal chop, a serving of mashed cauliflower and a serving of combined Brussels sprout fluff and burnt cherry rum shishito peppers - each on ⅓ of each plate

Herbed Veal Chop with Mashed Cauliflower, Brussels Sprout "Fluff" and Burnt Cherry Rum Shishito Peppers

Double Thick Pork Chop w/Hoisin Black Bean Brandy Marinade and Sauce, Lundberg Countrywild Rice and Garlic, Broccoli and Fennel with Crispy Fried Leeks

Time Line 1 hr.

Start 1 hr. before serving	15 min. after starting	30 min. after starting
Pork Chops 45 - 60 min.		marinate 30 min. minimum
Marinade and Sauce 30 min.	purée hoisin, beans and brandy 10 min.	
Rice 20 min.		
Vegetables 45 min.	peel, cut and prep vegetables 15 min.	parboil broccoli and fennel 15 min.
Garnish - Fried Leeks 30 min.		julienne leeks 15 min.

Cooking Hints

You can make extra marinade/sauce and keep refrigerated - to thin down for future use add more brandy
This marinade/sauce and the Crispy Fried Leeks works great on seabass (pg. 70)
Left over rice reheats nicely

Serves - 4

Double Thick Pork Chop
4 thick-cut, bone-in pork chops
 Marinade (30 min. minimum)
1 - 8 oz. jar Hoisin Sauce (Asian section
   supermarket)
1 - 15 oz. can black beans - drained
½ C. brandy - plus another 1 C. for sauce

Lundberg Countrywild Rice
2 C. chicken stock
1 Tbsp. olive oil
1 C. Lundberg Countrywild rice mix

Master Ingredient List

Garlic, Broccoli and Fennel
6 garlic cloves - peeled and diced fine
1 head broccoli - cleaned down to florets and
   cleaned and cut stems
1 C. cleaned fennel - large julienne
¼ C. olive oil

Garnish
1 large leek - cleaned, root end cut, up to green,
    - 3" julienne
1½ C. vegetable oil

Wine Suggestions
2016 Greywacke - Sauvignon Blanc $17
2015 Nikolaihof Smaragd Im Weingebirge
   Gruner Veltliner $21
2013 Zind Humbrecht, Domaine Heimbourg
   - Pinot Gris $50

Lundberg Countrywild Rice

Bring stock and oil to boil

Add rice

Bring back to boil and reduce heat until rice is done - 20 more min.+-

Keep warm until serving

Garlic, Broccoli and Fennel

Parboil cleaned trimmed broccoli/fennel mix for 10 min.

Drain and dry parboiled vegetables

In a hot frying pan (with lid) with olive oil sauté garlic 5-10 min.

Add broccoli and fennel - stir well and cover - shake or stir often

Cook for 15 min. - be ready to serve right away - (can wait until prior to serving to stir fry last 15 min.)

Crispy Fried Leeks

Heat vegetable oil to very hot in large saucepan

Place a handful at a time of the leeks in the hot oil

Cover with splatter screen and allow to cook until slightly brown

Remove fried leeks with slotted spoon and place in paper towel lined bowl to de-grease

Continue until all leeks are crispy fried

Double Thick Pork Chop

Purée hoisin sauce, black beans and ½ C. brandy until smooth

Marinate Pork in puréed mixture for minimum 30 min.

Remove chops from marinade and reserve marinade for sauce

Grill chops to desired doneness

Use an insta-read meat thermometer - pork should be at least 145°

...continued

30 min. before serving	15 min. before serving	**Serve** 1 hr. after starting

grill chops & 20 min.

cook sauce down 30 min.

boil rice 20 min.

sauté garlic, broccoli, fennel 30 min. total

fry leeks 15 min.

Hoisin Black Bean Brandy Sauce

Add 1 C. brandy to reserved marinade and heat in a saucepan

Bring marinade to a boil, cook off alcohol, and lower heat to simmer

Reduce marinade to thick sauce consistency - 10-15 min.

Plate

Place a double thick pork chop on ⅓ of each plate

Place a serving of Lundberg Countrywild rice on ⅓ of plate

Place a serving of garlic, broccoli and fennel on ⅓ of plate

Garnish

Top pork chop with sauce

Top sauced pork chop with a handful of the crispy fried leeks

Double Thick Pork Chop with Hoisin Black Bean Brandy Sauce,
Lundberg Countrywild Rice and Garlic Broccoli Fennel
with Crispy Fried Leek Garnish

Marinated Flank Steak w/Port Mushrooms, Mashed Sweet Potatoes and Carrots Vichy

Time Line 3 hr.

Start 3 hr. before serving	45 min. after starting	1½ hr. after starting
Flank Steak 2½ hr.	prepare marinade 15 min.	marinate flank steak 2 hr.
Mushrooms 1¼ hr.	clean, slice mushrooms 15 min.	marinate mushrooms 15 min. minimum
Mashed Sweet Potatoes 60 min.	peel and cut sweet pots 15 min.	
Carrots Vichy 1 hr.		prep and cut carrots 15 min.

Cooking Hints

Flank steak can be prepped and marinated (frozen OK) well ahead of time and grilled (thawed) just prior to serving
Any mushrooms can be used. Any stock can be used
You can make your own raspberry vinegar - boil frozen raspberries with white vinegar - strain after boiling

Serves - 4

Master Ingredient List

Flank Steak
In a ziploc bag combine:
1 flank steak
  Marinade (2 hr. minimum)
½ C. olive oil
½ C. teriyaki soy sauce
½ C. tequila
2 Tbsp. ginger root - skinned, finely diced
2 garlic cloves - peeled and minced
1 tsp. mustard powder

Port Mushrooms
1 lb. crimini mushrooms - cleaned, stemmed, sliced
1 C. beef stock reduced to thick syrup consistency
1 C. cheap port - I use jug tawny

Mashed Sweet Potatoes
4 large sweet potatoes - peeled and cut to
    2" chunks
2 Tbsp. butter
salt and pepper to taste

Carrots Vichy
6-10 carrots - peeled and cut to batonnets - ¼" x ¼" x 3"
3 Tbsp. butter
½ C. white sugar
1 C. water
½ C. raspberry vinegar

Wine Suggestions
2015 Bodegas Borsao Tres Picos - Grenache $13
2008 La Rioja Alta Vina Ardanza Reserva $24
2014 Quilceda - Creek Columbia Valley Red $42

Port Mushrooms

Marinate prepped sliced mushrooms in port for at least 30 min.

Add mushrooms and port to sauce pan with reduced stock

Cook in covered saucepan for at least 30 min. - make sure does
    not cook dry - if it does add more port

Remove lid, continue to cook until liquid is thick and almost gone

Keep warm until serving

Mashed Sweet Potatoes

Boil large pot of water

Salt and pepper to taste

Add prepped sweet potato chunks

Boil until soft

Drain and mash

Add butter and mix

...continued

		grill flank steak 15 min.	rest and slice 15 min.
cook mushrooms 45 min.			
boil sweet potatoes 30 min.		mash sweet potatoes 15 min.	
cook carrots 45 min.			

Carrots Vichy

Combine all prepped carrot ingredients in saucepan

Bring to boil, then simmer on medium until carrots are cooked crunchy

Liquid should thicken throughout cooking

Garnish with parsley or cilantro

Marinated Flank Steak

Allow steak and all steak ingredients to marinate at least 2 hr. (can leave in fridge for up to 3 days or freeze)

Grill steak to desired doneness - use an insta-read meat thermometer to check - rare 125°, medium 145°, well 160°

Slice on bias and arrange on plate in a fan

Plate

Place a serving of fanned sliced marinated flank steak over bottom ½ of each plate

Place a serving of port mushrooms over top of steak

Add a serving of mashed sweet potatoes to top quarter of plate - left side

Add a serving of carrots Vichy to top quarter of plate - right side

Marinated Flank Steak with Port Mushrooms, Mashed Sweet Potatoes and Sambuca Tarragon Cherry Tomatoes (pg. 42)

Degree of Difficulty   1/4

Spicy Grilled Chicken w/Baked Potatoes and Grilled Mixed Vegetables

Time Line 3 hr.

Start 3 hr. before serving	30 min. after starting	1 hr. after starting
Chicken 1-2 hr.	trim and rinse chicken 15 min.	marinate chicken 30 - 60 min.
Grilled Vegetables 1 hr.		clean and slice vegetables 30 min.
Mashed cauliflower 45 min.		
Chicken marinade into sauce 30 min.		

Cooking Hints

Chicken can be prepped ahead - frozen until needed.
Mashed cauliflower leftovers can be reheated.

Serves - 4

Master Ingredient List

Spicy Grilled Chicken
4 chicken breasts - boneless and
 skinless, trimmed of fat
 Marinade (30 min. minimum)
1 C. olive oil
1 C. brandy
½ C. sesame oil
4 Tbsp. hot sauce
2 Tbsp. dried chili pepper flakes
4 Tbsp. dried cilantro
2 Tbsp. sesame seeds

Baked Potatoes
4 baked potatoes
tinfoil for each potato
butter, sour cream, bacon bits - for garnish

Grilled Mixed Vegetables
4 carrots - scrubbed clean, sliced lengthwise ¼"
12 asparagus spears - cleaned and snapped
3 corn on the cob - cut in half and sliced
 length wise ½"

Grilled Mixed Vegetables...cont.
½ C. olive oil
salt and pepper to taste

Garnish
marinade reduced to sauce
dried cilantro

Wine Suggestions
2014 Conundrum - Proprietary Blend $16
2015 Brewer-Clifton Santa Rita Hills - Chardonnay $28
2014 Hilt Old Guard - Chardonnay $44

Baked Potatoes
Preheat oven to 350°

Scrub clean each potato (do not peel)

Wrap individually in tinfoil

Place in oven for at least 60 min.

Remove from tinfoil and cut a long "X" into the top of each potato

Squeeze the "X" to open the potato

Top with butter, sour cream, bacon bits

Grilled Mixed Vegetables
Preheat grill to high

Toss carrots, asparagus and corn cob in olive oil
 (can be mixed together)

Grill all vegetables on hot grill until desired doneness - asparagus
 will cook fastest, then carrots, corn last (about 15 min.+-)

Salt and pepper to taste

Keep warm until serving

...continued

1 hr. before serving		30 min. before serving		**Serve** 2 hr. after starting
marinate chicken 30 - 60 min.				grill chicken 15 - 30 min.
marinate vegetables 30 min.				grill vegetables 15 min.+-
trim cauliflower 15 min.		boil and mash cauliflower 30 min.		
		cook down chicken marinade to sauce 30 min.		

Spicy Grilled Chicken

Add trimmed and rinsed chicken breasts to ziploc bag containing all chicken Marinade ingredients

Marinate chicken for at least 30 min. - longer is fine - reserve marinade for sauce

Preheat grill to high

Grill chicken until desired doneness

Use an insta-read meat thermometer - chicken should be at least 160°

Sauce

Place marinade into saucepan and reduce to thick sauce consistency - 30 min.+-

Plate

Either leave whole or slice grilled chicken breasts

Place grilled chicken or breast slices, (1 breast/serving) a dressed baked potato and grilled mixed vegetables - each on ⅓ of each plate

Garnish

Top chicken with reduced marinade sauce

Sprinkle dried cilantro over plate

Spicy Grilled Chicken

Stacked Chicken Breast (Topped w/Eggplant, Chevre and Pesto) w/Rossa Risotto and Sesame Steamed Snow Peas

Time Line 2 hr.

Start 2 hr. before serving	30 min. after starting	1 hr. after starting
Chicken 1 hr.	trim and rinse chicken 15 min.	assemble chicken stack 15 min.
Eggplant 45 min.	clean, slice, oil and cinnamon and marinate eggplant 30 min.	grill eggplant 15 min.
Risotto 30-40 min.		

Cooking Hints

Risotto can be half cooked ahead and finished just prior to serving

Serves - 4

Stacked Chicken Breast
4 chicken breasts - boneless and skinless,
    trimmed of fat
2 Tbsp. olive oil
1 eggplant sliced lengthwise ½" thick
    - 1 slice/serving
4 Tbsp. olive oil - 1 Tbsp./slice of eggplant
4 Tbsp. cinnamon - 1 Tbsp./slice of eggplant
8 Tbsp. chevre cheese softened
    (use 2 oz./breast)
9 Tbsp. pesto (2 Tbsp./chicken breast) plus
    extra for garnish

Master Ingredient List

Rossa Risotto
2 C. stock (chicken or vegetable is best)
1 onion - peeled and finely diced
2 Tbsp. olive oil
1 C. Arborio rice
½ C. red wine
1 head radicchio lettuce finely shredded
½ C. grated hard cheese (Parm, Romano, or Asiago)

Sesame Steamed Snow Peas
2 C. snow peas - washed and ends trimmed
4 tsp. sesame oil

Wine Suggestions
2013 Robert Stemmler - Pinot Noir $18
2014 Domaine Drouhin Willamette Valley
    - Pinot Noir $31
2013 Domaine Jean Grivot Vosne Romanee
    - Pinot Noir $54

Rossa Risotto

Preheat the stock

Sauté the onion in olive oil until cooked and starting to color

Add unrinsed Arborio rice to sautéed onions and mix in well - when almost dry, add red wine and stir in well

Add half of the hot stock and stir well - cover and let sit on medium heat for 15 min. - reduce heat to low

Stir in shredded radicchio lettuce

30 min. prior to serving raise heat to medium high and add 2nd half of hot stock - stir into rice mixture and cover

Mix in cheese

Keep warm until serving

Sesame Steamed Snow Peas

In a small saucepan with cover add:
2 C. water
Sesame oil
Snow peas

Bring to boil and turn off heat

Let sit for 15 min. with heat off - covered

Drain

Salt and pepper to taste

Keep warm until serving

...continued

| 1 hr. before serving | | 30 min. before serving | | Serve 2 hr. after starting |

bake chicken stack 30 min.

make risotto 45 min.

Stacked Chicken Breast

Heat grill to high

Preheat oven to 300°

Paint sliced eggplant with olive oil - both sides

Sprinkle cinnamon on oil painted eggplant - both sides - let eggplant sit for 20 min.

Grill eggplant 7 min.+- per side

Rub chicken breasts with olive oil - salt and pepper chicken breast to taste

Top chicken breast with chevre cheese - spread over top of breast

Place grilled eggplant on top of chevre cheese

Spread pesto over eggplant

Place stacked chicken breast, chevre, eggplant, pesto in heated oven for 30 min.

Use an insta-read meat thermometer - chicken should be at least 160°

Plate

Place 1 stacked chicken breast (cut in half), a serving of rossa risotto and a serving of sesame steamed snow peas - each on ⅓ of each plate

Garnish

Dab open areas of plate with small pesto drops

Stacked Chicken Breast ,with Eggplant, Chevre and Pesto

Stuffed Chicken Breast (Stuffed with Prosciutto, Spinach, Swiss Cheese) w/Grand Marnier Cream Sauce, Garlic Sage Roasted Fingerling Potatoes and Tofu Snap Peas

Time Line 2 hr.

Start 2 hr. before serving	30 min. after starting	1 hr. after starting
Chicken 1 hr.	trim, rinse, slice chicken 10 min.	assemble stuffed chicken 15 min.
Spinach 15 min.	wash and sauté spinach 15 min.	
Tofu Snap Peas 30 min.	prep and marinate tofu 30 min.	
Potatoes 60 min.	prep garlic and potatoes 15 min.	parboil potatoes 15 min.
Grand Marnier Sauce 30-45 min.		

Cooking Hints

Try low sodium and or gluten-free soy for the tofu marinade
Don't be afraid to try different cheeses

Serves - 4

Master Ingredient List

Stuffed Chicken Breast
4 chicken breasts - boneless and skinless,
    trimmed of fat
1 bag spinach
¼ lb. butter
1 tsp. fresh ground nutmeg
4 slices prosciutto
4 slices Swiss cheese

Garlic Sage Roasted Fingerling Potatoes
12 fingerling potatoes - cleaned and cut in half
1 Tbsp. olive oil
3 garlic cloves - peeled and diced small
¼ C. fresh sage (use less if dried)

Tofu Snap Peas
1 C. soy sauce
½ C. ginger - skinned and diced small
2 garlic cloves - peeled and diced small
1 lb. firm tofu - cut into ½" cubes
½ C. oil (frying)
1 lb. sugar snap peas - washed and stems
    snipped

Grand Marnier Cream Sauce
1 C. Grand Marnier or other orange
    liqueur
1 C. heavy cream

Garnish
¼ C. grated orange zest

Wine Suggestions
2014 Casanova di Neri Irrosso di
    - Sangiovese Blend $15
2010 San Gregorio, Feudi di Taurasi Riserva Piano
    di Montevergine - Proprietary Blend $29
2013 Robert Keenan - Cabernet Franc $55

Garlic Sage Roasted Fingerling Potatoes

Preheat oven to 350°

Clean and scrub fingerling potatoes

Parboil in salted and peppered water until soft 10 min.+-

Drain and dry potatoes and toss in a bowl with olive oil

Add garlic and sage and continue to toss

Place in baking dish, tinfoil cover and place in 350° oven for 30 min.

Remove tinfoil and bake another 15 min.

Tofu Snap Peas

Marinate tofu cubes in soy sauce, ginger and garlic for 30 min.

Heat ½ C. oil very hot in large saucepan

Tofu Snap Peas...cont.

Stir fry tofu until crisp on all sides - remove and drain

Add snap peas to hot oil and stir fry

Add crisp, drained tofu and mix well while keeping hot

Keep warm until serving

Grand Marnier Cream Sauce

Combine Grand Marnier or other orange liqueur and heavy cream
    and bring to a boil

Lower heat and reduce to sauce consistency

Add ½ of the grated orange zest

1 hr. before serving	30 min. before serving	Serve 2 hr. after starting

bake stuffed chicken 30 min.

roast potatoes 45 min.+-

cook and reduce Grand Marnier sauce 30 min.+-

Stuffed Chicken Breast

Preheat oven to 300°

Sauté spinach in butter and add grated nutmeg

Slice breast in half through the thickness

Layer a slice of prosciutto over top of chicken breast

Layer a slice of Swiss cheese over top of chicken breast

Top with sautéed spinach evenly over Swiss cheese

Roll breast into a log - you can use picks, skewers or butcher elastic mesh to hold log together

Place chicken logs in baking dish and cook for 30 min. or to desired doneness

Use an insta-read meat thermometer - chicken should be at least 160°

Plate

Cut cooked stuffed chicken breast into 1" slices and place a serving, (½ breast per serving) cut side up, on ⅓ of each plate

Place a serving of garlic sage roasted fingerling potatoes on ⅓ of plate

Place serving of tofu snap peas on ⅓ of plate

Garnish

Drizzle Grand Marnier sauce over chicken slices

Top plate with grated orange zest

Chicken Breast Stuffed With Prosciutto, Spinach and Swiss Cheese Topped with Grand Marnier Cream Sauce

Boneless Stuffed Cornish Hens w/Lobster Risotto and Steamed Broccoli

Time Line 3 hr.

Start 3 hr. before serving	45 min. after starting	1½ hr. after starting
Cornish Hens 2 hr.	remove bones from Cornish hens 1 hr.	
Broccoli 30 min.		
Risotto 45 min.		make risotto 45 min.
Lobster 20 min.		
Grand Marnier Basting Sauce 20 min.		cook sauce 20 min.

Cooking Hints

*To bone the hens, and stuff the hens, watch the "How To" videos on our website - **www.boozehoundsguidetogourmet.com***
This is a lot of work - make the most of it and do more than 2 hens at a time - they freeze well, even when boned

Serves - 4

Boneless Stuffed Cornish Hens
2 Cornish hens boned as in video
   www.boozehoundsguidetogourmet.com
1 Tbsp. olive oil
salt and pepper to taste
butcher elastic mesh, string or metal oven picks

Broccoli
1 large head broccoli - cleaned, cut to florets
        and stems trimmed to batons
1 Tbsp. truffle oil

Master Ingredient List

Lobster Risotto
2 lobster tails - shelled and cut into ½" cubes
2 Tbsp. butter - for sautéing lobster
¼ C. Grand Marnier or other orange liqueur - for
        sautéing lobster
1 onion - peeled and finely diced
2 Tbsp. olive oil
1 C. arborio rice
½ C. white wine
2 C. stock (chicken or vegetable is best)
½ C. grated hard cheese (Parm, Romano,Asiago)

Sauce
1 C. Grand Marnier or other orange liqueur
1 - 10 oz. jar orange marmalade

Wine Suggestions
2013 Emmolo - Sauvignon Blanc $16
2014 Hermann Donnhoff Oberhauser Brucke
        - Riesling $35
2013 Domaine Grillot et Bitouzet Meursaul
        Perrières - Chardonnay $55

Lobster
Heat butter in saucepan large enough to hold lobster

Add lobster pieces - stirring constantly

Add orange liqueur and allow to flame and burn off

Continue cooking until lobster is done - 3-5 min.

Keep warm until adding to risotto

Steamed Broccoli
Add truffle oil to pot of boiling water

Add broccoli pieces to steamer over boiling oiled water
        - cover and let steam

Remove from heat when broccoli is done - 10-15 min.

Keep warm until serving

Basting Sauce
Combine orange liqueur and orange marmalade

Boil and reduce to thin sauce consistency

Lobster Risotto
Preheat the stock

Sauté the onion in olive oil until cooked and starting to color

Add un-rinsed arborio rice to onions and mix in well - when almost
        dry, add white wine and stir in well

Add half of the hot stock and stir well - cover and let sit on medium
        heat for 15 min. then reduce heat to low

30 min. prior to serving raise heat to medium high and add 2nd
        half of hot stock - stir into rice mixture and cover

Mix in cheese and mix in cooked lobster - allow to cool prior to
        stuffing

Boneless Stuffed Cornish Hens
Watch the video on our website to see how to stuff these hens
        www.boozehoundsguidetogourmet.com

Preheat oven to 350°

Stuff boned Cornish hens with cooled lobster risotto

...continued

1¼ hr. before serving		45 min. before serving		Serve 3 hr. after starting
	stuff hens with lobster risotto and bind 30 min.		bake stuffed hens 30 - 60 min.	
		clean, trim, broccoli 15 min.	steam broccoli 15 min.	
make risotto 45 min.				
shell, cut and cook lobster 20 min.				

Boned Cornish Hen...cont.

Place stuffed hen in butcher elastic mesh and tie ends, or tie or skewer ends closed with pick

Place stuffed and tied hens on baking rack on baking sheet or pan

Place in oven and baste with reduced Grand Marnier or other orange liqueur/ orange marmalade sauce

Continue to baste every 15 min.

Remove from oven when internal temperature is 160°

Allow to rest out of heat for 15 min.

Plate

Cut hens in half (each half gets a leg, breast and wing) being careful to not let stuffing fall out

Place each halved hen centered on each plate - cut side down, skin side up

Place steamed broccoli pieces around plated hen halves

Garnish

Drizzle any remaining basting sauce over top of hen halves

Boneless, Lobster Risotto Stuffed Cornish Hens
Ready to go in the oven (in butcher elastic mesh)
Use a Grand Marnier baste

Half of a Boneless, Lobster Risotto Stuffed Cornish Hen
(Plate like this)

61

Turducken (Boned, Stuffed, Turkey, Duck, Chicken) w/Oyster Bourbon Cornbread Stuffing, Dirty Mashed Potatoes and Carrots

Time Line 5 hr.

Start- 5 hr. before serving		1½ hr. after starting		2½ hr. after starting
Turkey,Duck,Chicken 4 hr.	bone birds 30 min.	assemble 30 min.	cook Turducken to desired doneness 3 hr.+-	
Oysters 30 min.	clean,cut,fry 30 min.			
Cornbread 45 min.	mix, bake and cool 40 min.			
Dirty Mashed Potatoes 1 hr.	scrub, boil, mash 1 hr.			
Gravy 2 hr.	cook down stock and au jus 2 hr. +-			
Carrots 20 min.	clean, peel, cut, parboil 20 min.			

Cooking Hints

This is a lot of work and a lot of food - make the most of it and prepare this for a large group and be ready to spend most of the day doing it!
Make a stock from all the bones, add onion, carrot, garlic, then reduce, for a gravy or "au jus" **Best cooking method is in a turkey roaster**

Serves - 8 to 10

Turkey, Duck and Chicken
1 - boned, opened up chicken
1 - boned, opened up duck - larger than chicken
1 - boned, opened up turkey - larger than duck
½ Tbsp. olive oil per bird
salt and pepper to taste
butcher elastic mesh or string or metal oven picks

Dirty Mashed Potatoes
5 lb. bag potatoes - scrubbed and cut into
          1" chunks - DO NOT PEEL potatoes
3 quarts chicken stock
water to cover potatoes/stock in large stock pot

Carrots
10 large carrots - washed, peeled, cut 3" X ¼" X ¼"

Master Ingredient List

Oyster Bourbon Cornbread Stuffing
1½ C. finely ground yellow cornmeal
½ C. all-purpose flour or gluten-free flour
¼ C. granulated sugar
1½ tsp. baking powder
1 tsp. fine salt
1 C. whole milk
½ C. bourbon
2 large eggs
¼ C. olive oil to fry oysters
6 shucked oysters - rinsed, cut to ¼" pieces, fried
6 Tbsp. unsalted butter, melted, plus more for
          coating the baking dish

Gravy/Au Jus
all of the bones from boning the birds

Gravy/Au Jus...cont.
stockpot of potato boiling liquid
1 C. white wine
1 onion - peeled and finely diced
2 large carrots - peeled and finely diced
3 garlic cloves - peeled and finely diced
1 tsp. salt and ½ tsp. pepper

Wine Suggestions
2013 Podere Poggio Scalette Chianti Classico
          - Sangiovese $13
2015 Nikolaihof Federspiel Vom Stein
          - Riesling $24
2011 Ciacci Piccolomini d'Aragona Brunello di
          Montalcino - Sangiovese $36

Oyster Bourbon Cornbread Stuffing

Heat the oven to 425° and arrange a rack in the middle

Coat 8" X 8" baking dish with butter and set aside

Place the cornmeal, flour, sugar, baking powder and salt in a large
          bowl and whisk to combine

Place milk, eggs and bourbon in a medium bowl and whisk until
          eggs are broken up

Pour milk mixture into cornmeal mixture - stir until incorporated

Stir in the melted butter until incorporated without streaks of butter

Add fried oyster bits and mix in

Pour mixture into the prepared baking dish

Bake until golden brown around the edges and a toothpick inserted
          into the center comes out clean, about 20-25 min.

Oyster Bourbon Cornbread Stuffing...cont.

Remove the dish to a wire rack and let cool for at least 15 min.

When cool - break up to spread on top of turkey layer

Dirty Mashed Potatoes

Boil potatoes in stockpot with chicken stock - top up stock with
          water as needed to cover potatoes

When boiled soft, drain and mash - reserve liquid

Salt and pepper to taste

When cooled - spread ½" layer on top of duck layer

Carrots

Parboil prepped carrots in water - 10 min.

Place parboiled carrots on chicken layer

...continued

cook Turducken to desired doneness 3 hr.+-   - rest 20 min. prior to cutting and serving

Gravy/Au Jus

Boil all ingredients for gravy/au jus - for at least an hour.

Strain bones out and purée liquid stock and onion, carrots, garlic

Return to heat and reduce to thick gravy consistency

Turkey, Duck, Chicken (Turducken)

Preheat oven or turkey roaster to 400°

Lay out flat boned, opened turkey on a large baking sheet

Place cornbread mixture all over turkey layer ½" thick - reserve any remaining cornbread for table service

Place boned, opened, duck on top of cornbread

Place dirty mashed potato mixture all over duck layer ½" thick - reserve any remaining mashed potatoes for table service

Place boned, opened, chicken on top of mashed potato

Place parboiled carrots on top of chicken - reserve any remaining carrots for table service

Roll up turducken and bind with large butcher elastic mesh, or string or metal oven picks - this is at least a 2 person job

The idea is to have the whole works rolled up to look somewhat like a regular stuffed turkey

Place turducken in oven on a rack in a large baking sheet, or into turkey roaster (better method)

Bast with gravy/au jus often

Cook to desired doneness. Use an insta-read meat thermometer - poultry should be at least 160°

Remove from heat and let rest for 20 min.

Plate

Slice the cooked/rested turducken in full slices, and place on the center of each plate

The idea is to have a slice with rings of each layer: from the inside out : carrots, chicken, mashed potatoes, duck, cornbread stuffing, turkey

Don't forget to remove the binding (*butcher elastic mesh, string, whatever you used*) prior to plating

Garnish

Drizzle gravy/au jus over everything

Turducken in the Serving Tray

63

Duck Breast (w/Chinese 4 Spice) w/Raspberry Port Sauce, Jasmine Rice, and Sesame Grilled Asparagus

Time Line 1½ hr.

Start 3 hr. before serving	30 min. after starting	45 min. after starting
Duck Breast 60 min. +-	trim excess fat, cross hatch skin 15 min.	marinate duck 30 min. minimum
Jasmine Rice 15 min.		
Asparagus. 20-30 min.	clean and prep asparagus 15 min.	
Sauce 30 min.		

Cooking Hints

These duck breasts can marinate longer than specified - refrigerate during marinating
The duck can be served with the fat cap still on
Chinese 4 spice is equal parts of: cinnamon, white pepper, nutmeg and ginger - minimum 1 tsp. of each

Serves - 4

Duck Breast
4 duck breasts with fat cap still on
Marinade (30 min. minimum)
2 Tbsp. Chinese 4 spice mixture
1 C. port

Jasmine Rice
2 C. chicken stock
2 Tbsp. butter
1 C. Jasmine rice

Master Ingredient List

Sesame Grilled Asparagus
20 asparagus spears - cleaned and snapped
½ C. sesame oil

Raspberry Port Sauce
left over marinade from duck breasts
1 - 10-12 oz. package frozen raspberries
½ C. port
sugar to taste

Garnish
fresh raspberries
raspberry port sauce

Wine Suggestions
2011 Hop Kiln (HKG) - Pinot Noir $15
2014 Maison L'Envoye The Attache
        - Pinot Noir $25
2014 Melville Block M - Pinot Noir $49

Jasmine Rice

Bring stock and butter to boil in covered saucepan

Add rice to boiling stock, stir and cover

When water/rice boils - reduce heat to low, cook covered
        for 15 min.

Keep warm until serving

Sesame Grilled Asparagus

Marinate asparagus and sesame oil in a ziploc bag

Heat grill to hot

Place asparagus on hot grill until done - 5-10 min.

Keep warm until serving

Duck Prep and Marinade

Score duck fat in hash X marks - not quite all the way through the fat

Rub duck with 4 spice mix

Pour port into bottom of baking dish with sides

Place 4 spiced rubbed duck into port - fat side down for 30 min.

Raspberry Port Sauce

Combine marinade and thawed berries

Add ½ C. port

Heat and reduce to thick sauce consistency

Sweeten with sugar to taste

Keep warm until serving

...continued

45 min. before serving	30 min. before serving	Serve 1½ hr. after starting

cook duck 30 min.

cook Jasmine rice 15 min. and keep warm until serving

steam asparagus 10 min. +-

cook and reduce sauce 20 - 30 min.

Duck Breast Cooking

Preheat oven to 300°

Remove duck from marinade - reserve marinade
  - pat duck dry

Bake at 300° - 30 min. on a rack

Remove from oven and let rest 15 min.

Slice cooked duck breasts very thin (you can keep fat on
  duck if desired)

Plate

Fan out duck slices on bottom ½ of each plate
  (1 sliced breast/serving)

Place 5 sesame grilled asparagus spears on ½ of upper part
  of plate- left side

Place a serving of Jasmine rice ½ of upper part of plate
  - right side

Garnish

Drizzle raspberry port sauce over duck

Garnish plate with fresh berries

Chinese 4 Spice Duck, Raspberry Port Sauce,
Lundberg CountryWild Rice (pg. 50) and Cheesy Asparagus (pg. 34)

Seabass Mariscada (A One Pot Dinner for 4)

Time Line 1 hr.

Start 1 hr. before serving			30 min. after starting
Prep all items 20 min.	prep and clean all items 20 min.		
Seabass 30 min.		sear fish in oil 10 min.	
Cook all items 40 min.			cook vegetables and final cook fish 40 min.
Cook Sauce 20 min.			

Cooking Hints

This is an easy classy dinner that works well with any firm white fish. I use seabass, but try other firm white fish
Reheat refrigerated leftovers for a great 2nd round
You can use leftover sauce as a base for other things - see photo pg. 75

Serves - 4

Seabass Mariscada
4 - 6-8 oz. fillets - white, dense fish such as sea bass
½ C. olive oil or butter
2 onions - peeled and cubed
4 garlic cloves - peeled and minced
1 shallot - peeled and sliced thin
4 carrots - peeled and diced
4 sweet potatoes - peeled and cubed
4 C. chicken stock
1 C. white wine
4 peppers (red, green, yellow) - cleaned and cubed
1 stalk fennel - chopped

Master Ingredient List

Seabass Mariscada...cont.
2 stalks lemon grass - sliced up to woody part, or 1 lemon rind julienned
4 tomatoes - peeled, seeded and cubed

Garnish
lemon zest
Mariscada sauce

Wine Suggestions
Chardonnay
2013 Mer Soleil Silver Unoaked - Chardonnay $16
2015 Paul Hobbs Russian River Valley Crossbarn - Chardonnay $25
2014 Shafer - Chardonnay $47

Seabass Mariscada

Quickly sear all sides of fish in large saucepan in ¼ C. olive oil

Remove fish from pan and set aside - covered with foil

Add 2 Tbsp. butter and sauté onion, garlic and shallots

Add carrots, sweet potatoes, 2 C. chicken stock and 1 C. white wine

Simmer, covered for 20 min. or until sweet potatoes are just done

Add peppers, fennel and lemon grass, or lemon rind

Add 2 C. of chicken stock - simmer, covered, for another 10 min.

Seabass Mariscada...cont.

Add fish to middle of pan and simmer, covered - for a further 10 min.

Add tomatoes 5 min. before done

With a ladle or strainer, remove as much liquid from the saucepan as you can

Keep saucepan contents warm until plating - in oven at 170°

Seabass Mariscada Sauce

In a separate pot, heat the removed liquid from above, and reduce until quite thick and use as final sauce

...continued

Serve 1 hr. after starting

cook vegetables and final cook fish 40 min.

cook sauce 20 min.

Plate

Remove lemon grass if used - if lemon peel used leave it in

Place a fish fillet centered on each plate

Spoon mixture of vegetables over fish

Garnish

Spoon reduced mariscada sauce over top of fish and
vegetables

Top everything with lemon zest

*Seabass Mariscada with Fennel, Onion,Peppers,
Tomatoes and Sweet Potatoes*

Grilled Mahi-Mahi w/Tequila Jalapeño Cilantro Glaze, Baked Sweet Potato Fries and Roasted Truffle Brussels Sprouts

Time Line 1½ hr.

Start 1 hr. before serving	15 min. after starting	45 min. after starting
Brussels Sprouts 30 min.		prep Brussels sprouts 10-15 min.
Sweet Potato Fries 1¼ hr.	peel and cut sweet potato fries 30 min.	
Mahi-Mahi 30 min.		
Cilantro Jalapeño Glaze 20 min.	cook glaze ingredients (except agave) 20 min.	purée 10 min.

Cooking Hints

This works with any fish
Make enough dill Hollandaise to have leftovers - refrigerates well

Serves - 4

Grilled Mahi-Mahi
4 - 6-8 oz. fillets Mahi-Mahi - boned and skinned
olive oil to coat fish
salt and pepper to taste

Baked Sweet Potato Fries
2 large sweet potatoes - cleaned, peeled, cut into "French fry" shape -
¼ C. olive oil
salt and pepper to taste

Master Ingredient List

Roasted Truffle Brussels Sprouts
1 lb. Brussels sprouts - cleaned and cut in half
¼ C. truffle oil

Tequila Jalapeño Cilantro Glaze
2-3 bunches fresh cilantro - rinsed
3-4 Jalapeños - cleaned and diced fine
4 garlic cloves - peeled and diced fine
12 oz. lime juice - fresh squeezed or bottled Key Lime
½ C. tequila
6-12 oz. agave, or other sweetener - to taste - not too tart, not too sweet

Wine Suggestions
2014 Landmark Overlook - Chardonnay $18
2015 Delille Cellars Chaleur Estate Blanc - Sémillon-Sauvignon Blanc Blend $35
2015 Tor Kenward Durell Vineyard - Chardonnay $60

Baked Sweet Potato Fries
Preheat oven to 350°

Toss cut sweet potatoes in olive oil and place on baking sheet - single layer thick

Salt and pepper to taste

Bake for 45 min. - more or less based on desired crispiness

Roasted Truffle Brussels Sprouts
Preheat oven to 350°

Toss prepped Brussels sprouts in a bowl with truffle oil

Place oiled Brussels sprouts on baking sheet - flat side down

Roast for 30-45 min. until tender but not mushy

Tequila Jalapeño Cilantro Glaze
Place cilantro, jalapeños, garlic, lime juice and tequila in saucepan and bring to boil

Reduce heat and simmer for another 15 min.

Let cool, then pour contents into blender, process until blended - strain

Return blended, strained contents back to saucepan and bring to boil

Add agave to bring the flavor to a combination of sweet, tart and spicy

Reduce to sauce consistency - be careful that as the sauce reduces, it's not too sweet

...continued

45 min. before serving	**Serve** 1 hr. after starting

roast Brussels sprouts 45+- min.

bake sweet potato fries 45 min.

clean and remove bones 15 min.	grill Mahi-Mahi 15 min.+-

reduce glaze 30 min.+-

Grilled Mahi-Mahi
Coat fish with olive oil

Salt and pepper to taste

Grill on hot grill - 5-7 min. per side (+- to suit doneness)

Plate
Place a grilled fish fillet, a serving of baked sweet potato
fries and a serving of roasted Brussels sprouts on
⅓ of each plate

Garnish
Top fish with tequila jalapeño cilantro glaze

*Grilled Mahi-Mahi with a Tequila, Jalapeño Cilantro Glaze,
Baked Sweet Potato Fries and Roasted Truffle Brussels Sprouts*

Grilled Seabass w/Hoisin Black Bean Brandy, Lundberg Countrywild Rice, Steamed Asparagus and Crispy Fried Leeks

Time Line 1 hr.

Start 1 hr. before serving		30 min. after starting
Crispy Leeks 30 min.	clean and Julienne leeks 15 min.	fry leeks 15 min.
Grilled Seabass 45 min.	purée marinade	marinate seabass in black bean hoisin brandy purée 30 min.
Black Bean Hoisin sauce 30 min.		
Lundberg Countrywild Rice 30 min.		cook wild rice 30 min.
Steamed Asparagus 15 min.	prep and marinate asparagus 10 min.	

Cooking Hints

Cook leeks first - they are fine as a cold garnish - you can also refrigerate any leftovers for future use
The seabass can be marinated for much longer if it suits your timing. While the seabass is marinating, refrigerate if longer than 30 min.
As soon as the asparagus reboils - turn off heat and let sit - this will cook fast! Leftover sauce will refrigerate well for later use - just thin with brandy. The marinade/sauce and Crispy Fried leeks works great on pork chops (pg. 50)

Serves - 4

Grilled Seabass
4 - 6-8 oz. fillets - sea bass
  Marinade/Sauce (30 min. minimum)
1 - 8 oz. jar Hoisin Sauce (Asian section supermarket)
1 - 15 oz. can black beans - drained
½ C. brandy - plus another 1 C. for sauce

Crispy Fried Leeks
1 large leek - cleaned, root end cut, up to green
    - 3" julienne
1½ C. vegetable oil

Master Ingredient List

Lundberg Countrywild Rice
2 C. chicken stock
2 Tbsp. butter
1 C. Lundberg Countrywild Rice mix

Steamed Asparagus
20 asparagus spears - cleaned and snapped
1 Tbsp. truffle oil
salt and pepper to taste

Wine Suggestions
2011 Gloria Ferrer Carneros - Pinot Noir $16
2013 Domaine Michel Niellon Chassagne
    Montrachet Rouge - Pinot Noir $29
2014 Goldeneye (Duckhorn) - Pinot Noir $39

Crispy Fried Leeks

Heat vegetable oil to very hot in large saucepan

Place a handful at a time of the leeks in the hot oil

Cover with splatter screen and allow to cook until slightly brown

Remove fried leeks with slotted spoon and place in paper
    towel lined bowl to de-grease

Continue until all leeks are crispy fried

Lundberg Countrywild Rice

Bring stock and oil to boil

Add rice to boiling stock

Bring back to boil and reduce heat until rice is done - 30 more
    min.+-

Keep warm until serving

Hoisin Black Bean Brandy Marinade

In a food processor - purée - black beans, hoisin sauce and ½ C.
    brandy

Marinate fish in above purée for at least 30 min.

After marinating fish, reserve marinade for Black Bean, Hoisin,
    Brandy Sauce

Steamed Asparagus

Place asparagus and truffle oil in ziploc bag for 10 min.

Place asparagus and truffle oil in steamer over water

Cover and bring to boil (allow truffle oil to drain into water)

Steam for 5-10 min.

...continued

| grill seabass 15+- min. |
| reduce marinade to sauce 10-15 min. |
| cook wild rice 30+- min. |
| steam asparagus 5-10 min. |

Black Bean, Hoisin, Brandy Sauce

Add 1 C. brandy to reserved marinade and heat in a saucepan

Bring marinade to a boil, cook off alcohol, and lower heat to simmer

Reduce marinade to thick sauce consistency - 10-15 min

Grilled Seabass

After marinating seabass for 30 min.+ - remove from marinade

Cook seabass on hot grill for 5-7 min./side or to desired doneness

Plate

Place each piece of grilled seabass, a serving of Lundberg Countrywild rice and a serving of steamed asparagus (5 spears) on ⅓ of each plate

Garnish

Spoon Black Bean, Hoisin, Brandy Sauce over fish

Top sauced fish with a handful of the crispy fried leeks

Garnish with dots of sauce around the plate

Grilled Seabass - Marinated in Black Bean, Hoisin, Brandy with Reduced Black Bean, Hoisin, Brandy Sauce, Garnished with Crispy Fried Leeks

Seafood en Papillote (Baked in a Paper Bag) w/Salmon, Shrimp, Scallops, Mushrooms, Broccoli, Potatoes, Carrots, Champagne Cream Sauce and Caviar

Time Line 1 hr.

Start 1 hr. before serving	15 min. after starting	30 min. after starting
Prep all 15 min.	prep all ingredients 15-20 min.	
Potatoes 10 min.		parboil potatoes 10 min.
Salmon 2-3 min.		heat salmon in bubbly 2 min.
Shrimp and Scallops 2 min.		heat shrimp and scallops in bubbly 1-2 min.
Assemble and Bake Bags 20 min.		
Champagne Cream Sauce 20-30 min.		

Cooking Hints

To see how to do this, watch the video on our website - **www.boozehoundsguidetogourmet.com**
Prep potatoes first to parboil ASAP. Heat salmon next so bag assembly can happen fast. You can use this cooking method for a variety of fish, meat and chicken , or just veggies too - and with other sauce and garnish ideas. This is served best with a helper - one of you to cut open the bag - and the other one to pour sauce and a dollop of caviar into each "papillote"

Serves - 4

Master Ingredient List

Salmon and Seafood
4 - 6-8 oz. salmon fillet - boned/skinned
8 large scallops - washed
12 large shrimp - peeled and deveined
1 bottle cheap bubbly

Vegetables
4 very large mushrooms - cleaned, stemmed
1 broccoli head - washed and cut up to florets
12 fingerling potatoes - washed and scrubbed
12 baby carrots - washed
1 C. sesame oil

Garnish
1 small jar black caviar
the Champagne Cream Sauce

For the Bags
20"-22" of parchment paper per serving
½ C. olive oil and a pastry brush or 1" paint brush

For the Sauce
the bubbly from parboiling seafood and veggies
½ qt. heavy cream
2 Tbsp. Coco Lopez (Cream of Coconut)

Wine Suggestions
Jansz Brut Rose Cuvee
        - Champagne Blend $20
Delamotte Blanc de Blancs
        -Champagne Blend $37
NV Veuve Clicquot Ponsardin Brut,
        - Champagne $60

Fingerling Potatoes
Parboil washed and scrubbed (not peeled) fingerling potatoes
    - 10 min. in bubbly

Place parboiled potatoes in large bowl w/1 Tbsp. sesame oil - toss

Baby Carrots
Parboil washed baby carrots - 10 min. in water - NOT bubbly!
    (carrots will stain the bubbly)

Place parboiled carrots in bowl w/1 Tbsp. sesame oil - toss

Add parboiled carrots to potato bowl and combine

Salmon
Parboil salmon in bubbly for 2 min.

Remove with slotted spoon

Place in bowl and toss w/1 Tbsp. sesame oil and gently mix

Keep salmon/sesame separate from vegetable bowl

Shrimp and Scallops
Parboil prepped shrimp and scallops in boiling bubbly 1-2 min.

Place shrimp and scallops in bowl w/2 Tbsp. sesame oil and toss

Add to potato, and carrot bowl

Mushrooms and Broccoli
Clean and stem mushrooms

Clean and trim broccoli - small florets and trim thick stems to batons
    ¼" X ¼" X 2"

Place mushrooms and broccoli in bowl w/2 Tbsp. sesame oil and toss

Add to potato, carrot, shrimp/scallop bowl

Set aside

Champagne Cream Sauce
After parboiling potatoes and heating seafood continue to boil
    bubbly

...continued

assemble baking bags 10 min.	bake assembled bags 10 min.
cook and reduce Champagne Sauce 20-30 min.	

Champagne Cream Sauce...cont.

When reduced to ⅓ volume, add cream and bring to boil

Continue to boil until reduced to thick sauce consistency at least 30 min.

Add Coco Lopez and continue to boil to bring taste to just shy of sweet - 15-20 min.+-

Assembly and Baking

Watch the video on our website to see how to build these "bags"
www.boozehoundsguidetogourmet.com

Preheat oven to 450°

Fold parchment paper in half across width and cut into elongated ovals

Place salmon on parchment - in middle against the fold

Arrange shrimp, scallops, mushroom, broccoli and potatoes on top of and around the salmon - keep as small a footprint as possible

Fold open half of parchment paper over top of half with items piled

Starting at one side of the curve, fold and wrap the two sides together

Continue around the oval curve

If need be, you can staple the ends so they don't open

Paint both sides of sealed bag with olive oil

Place on sheet in oven and bake for 10 min.

Plate Serve and Garnish

Place baked bag on center of a large plate (folded edges up like in the photo above)

Take baked bags to table and at each setting, cut each bag open with knife and scissors

Pour champagne cream sauce into each cut open bag

Place a dollop of caviar on top of sauce in each bag

Seafood en Papillote - Prior to Opening

Seafood en Papillote w/Salmon, Shrimp, Scallops, Mushrooms, Broccoli, Potatoes, Carrots, Champagne Cream Sauce and Caviar

Stuffed Grouper (Bacon Wrapped, Mushroom and Crab Stuffed) w/Dill Hollandaise Sauce, Sambuca Oyster Mushroom Risotto, and Baked Green Beans

Time Line 2 hr.

Start 2 hr. before serving	30 min. after starting	60 min. after starting
Stuffing 45 min.	prep stuffing ingredients, marinate mushrooms 15 min.	sauté stuffing ingredients 30 min.
Wrapped, Stuffed Grouper 45 min.		
Cilantro Jalapeño Glaze 20 min.	cook glaze ingredients (except agave) 20 min.	purée 10 min.
Oyster Mushrooms 1 hr.	clean, slice and marinate Oyster mushrooms 30 min.	
Baked Green Beans 15 min.	prep green beans 5 min.+-	
Risotto 30-40 min.		

Cooking Hints

*To see how to stuff and bacon wrap fish - watch the video on our website - **www.boozehoundsguidetogourmet.com***
You can use any firm white fish - also works great with Mahi-Mahi
Left over Dill Hollandaise keeps well in the refrigerator
This also works well on a bed of leftover Seabass Mariscada (pg. 66)

Serves - 4

Master Ingredient List

Grouper
2 fillets grouper (1lb. each+-) - boned, skinned
2 lbs. bacon - enough to completely wrap
    the fish "sandwich"

Grouper Stuffing
1 large onion - peeled and diced fine
2 garlic cloves - peeled and diced fine
1 lb. crimini mushrooms - cleaned, stemmed,
    sliced and diced fine
½ C. white wine
1 - 8 oz. can crab - drained, rinsed, cut up fine

Dill Hollandaise Sauce
¼ C. butter or non-dairy butter or olive oil

Dill Hollandaise Sauce...cont.
2 heaping Tbsp. Knorr Hollandaise powder
2 - 14 oz. cans coconut milk - shaken prior to opening
1 tube dill paste

Sambuca Oyster Mushrooms
1 lb. oyster mushrooms - cleaned and cut large dice
1 C. Sambuca

Risotto
2 Tbsp. olive oil
1 onion - peeled and finely diced
½ C. white wine
1 C. arborio rice

Risotto...cont.
2 C. stock (chicken or vegetable is best)
½ C. grated hard cheese (Parm, Romano, Asiago)

Baked Green Beans
1 lb. fresh green beans - trimmed and cleaned
¼ C. flavored oil - I use truffle oil
½ C. grated cheese - Parm, Romano, or Asiago

Wine Suggestions
2014 La Crema Sonoma Coast - Chardonnay $18
2014 J Vineyards - Chardonnay $24.
2013 Hanzell - Chardonnay $50

Dill Hollandaise Sauce

Melt or heat fat in large saucepan

When fat is hot, add Hollandaise powder and blend well

Add coconut milk to fat/Hollandaise mix - stir well

Add dill paste

Boil for 15 min. then simmer for 30 min.

Heat prior to using - (can refrigerate left overs in sealed container)

Sambuca Oyster Mushrooms

In a large bowl combine cut mushrooms and Sambuca

Marinate for at least 30 min.

In a large saucepan (with a lid) bring mushrooms and Sambuca to
    boil and cook covered for 15 min. **careful - it will flame up**

Uncover and cook until almost dry (add more Sambuca if
    mushrooms cook dry)

Sambuca Oyster Mushrooms...cont.

Set cooked mushrooms aside to add to cooked risotto

Risotto

Preheat the stock

Sauté the onion in olive oil until cooked and starting to color

Add un-rinsed Arborio rice to onions and mix in - when almost dry,
    add white wine and stir in well

Add half of the hot stock and stir well - cover and let sit on medium
    heat for 15 min. - then reduce heat to low

30 min. prior to serving raise heat to medium high and add 2nd half
    of hot stock - stir into risotto mixture and cover

Mix in cheese and mix in Sambuca oyster mushrooms

Keep warm until serving

...continued

60 min. before serving	30 min. before serving	**Serve** 2 hr. after starting

stuff grouper - create "sandwich" and wrap bacon 15 min.

bake grouper 45 min.+-

reduce glaze 30 min.+-

sauté oyster mushrooms 30 min.

bake green beans 15-20 min.

make risotto 45 min.

Baked Green Beans
Preheat oven to 350°

In large bowl place prepped green beans and flavored oil - 15 min.

Place beans on baking sheet and top with cheese

Bake for 15-20 min.

Stuffed Grouper
Watch the video on our website to see how to make this
www.boozehoundsguidetogourmet.com

Preheat oven to 350°

Marinate prepped mushrooms in the white wine for at least 15 min.

Sauté mushrooms, onion, garlic - until mushrooms cooked - 15-20 min.

Add crab and continue to sauté another 10 min.- mix sautéed ingredients well

Make a sandwich of the sautéed ingredients - between the 2 Grouper fillets

Wrap the grouper/stuffing with bacon - all around - use toothpick to hold ends of bacon to the fish

Place in preheated oven on a rack and cook until bacon is done - 45 min.+-

Plate
Slice baked stuffed grouper into 2" thick slices

Place 1 slice of grouper on ⅓ of each plate - cut side flat (this will show off the stuffing)

Place a serving of Sambuca oyster mushroom risotto on ⅓ of plate

Place a serving of the baked green beans on ⅓ of plate

Garnish
Top fish with dill hollandaise sauce

Bacon Wrapped, Crab and Mushroom, Stuffed Grouper on the rack - just out of the oven

Bacon Wrapped, Crab and Mushroom, Stuffed Grouper Plated on Leftover Seabass Mariscada Sauce (pg. 66)

Potato Crusted Salmon Fillet w/Grilled Sesame Brussels Sprouts and Truffled Corn

Time Line 1 hr.

Start 30 min. before serving	15 min. after starting	30 min. after starting

| Potatoes 15 min. | clean, peel and shred potatoes 10 min. | |

Salmon 20 min.+-

| Brussels Sprouts 30 min. | | prep and marinate Brussels sprouts 10-15 min. |

| Corn 30 min. | prep and marinate corn 10-15 min. | |

Cooking Hints

Don't be afraid to mix up the fish choices with many of the fish dishes
Use the grill pan shown on the opposite page - available from Amazon - flat side up and cover with baking sheet to steam

Serves - 4

Potato Crusted Salmon
1 large salmon fillet - boned, skinned, sliced in 4
2 large potatoes - peeled and shredded
½ C. vodka
1 C. olive oil

Truffled Corn
2 corn cobs cleaned, and kernels cut off the cob
½ C. truffle oil

Master Ingredient List

Grilled Sesame Brussels Sprouts
1 lb. Brussels sprouts - cleaned and cut in half
   (save good loose leaves, "fluff" pg. 48)
½ C. sesame oil
2 C. water in pourable container (for steaming)

Garnish
cocktail sauce

Wine Suggestions
2016 Cade - Sauvignon Blanc $26
2014 Staglin - Chardonnay $39
2014 Liquid Farm Golden Slope
   - Chardonnay $50

Potato Crusted Salmon

Combine shredded potato and vodka

Pack potato/vodka around salmon - compress tightly into salmon fillet

Heat oil to very hot in large pan

Slide potato crusted salmon into hot oil using a metal spatula

Cook each side for 6-10 min. - flip carefully with spatula when done

Remove and set on paper towel to de-grease

Truffled Corn

Marinate prepped corn in truffle oil for 15 min. minimum

Sauté corn in large covered pan - 10-15 min.

When done, set aside to combine with cooked Brussels sprouts

Grilled Sesame Brussels Sprouts

Marinate prepped Brussels sprouts in sesame oil 15 min.

Preheat lightly oiled flat grill pan to very hot

Place sprouts onto hot grill sheet surface

Flip sprout halves to flat side down

After 5 min. cover with baking sheet

Add water to create steam

If water evaporates - add more - 10-15 min. total

Remove from heat and add to cooked corn

...continued

30 min. before serving		Serve 1 hr. after starting

cook potato crusted salmon 20 min.

cook Brussels sprouts 15+- min.

cook corn 15+- min.

Plate

Place a serving of cooked potato crusted fish centered on each plate

Scatter a serving of grilled sesame Brussels sprouts and truffled corn around fish

Garnish

Dab cocktail sauce on plate

Drizzle small amount on potato crust

*The best grill pan
Flat Side and Grill Side*

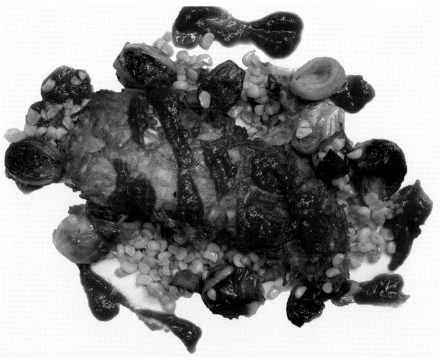

*Potato Crusted Salmon with
Grilled Sesame Brussels Sprouts and Truffled Corn*

Sesame Brussels Sprouts on the grill pan

Garlic and Clams Spaghetti

Time Line ½ hr.

Start 30 min. before serving	15 min. after starting	Serve 30 min. after starting
Garlic, Clams, Peppers 30 min.	prep all ingredients 10 min.	cook all ingredients 20 min.
Pasta 15 min.		cook pasta 15 min.

Cooking Hints

Works great with gluten-free pasta too
This is an easy and satisfying dish
Great for leftovers

Serves - 4

Garlic and Clams Spaghetti
1 lb. spaghetti

2 garlic cloves - peeled and minced
1 - 6-8 oz. can chopped clams
2 Tbsp. olive oil
½ C. white wine
1 red bell pepper - cleaned and diced
Parmesan cheese to taste

Master Ingredient List

Garnish
dried parsley
additional grated cheese

Wine Suggestions
2014 Bertani Velante - Pinot Grigio $12
2015 Chateau Montelena Potter Valley - Riesling $21
2016 Rombauer - Chardonnay $36

Garlic and Clams Spaghetti

Bring pasta to boil, and simmer, covered for 10 min. until al dente

Sauté garlic, clams and white wine in oil

Add red peppers

Toss sauté mixture with cooked and drained pasta

Stir in ½ of cheese with pasta/sauté mixture

Plate

Place a serving of mixed pasta centered on each plate

Garnish

Top pasta with dried parsley and additional cheese

Garlic and Clams Spaghetti

Penne w/Vodka, Tomato and Shrimp

Time Line ½ hr.

Start 30 min. before serving	15 min. after starting	Serve 30 min. after starting
Garlic, Tomatoes, Shrimp 30 min.	prep all ingredients 10 min.	cook all ingredients 20 min.
Pasta 15 min.	cook pasta 15 min.	
		combine everything

Cooking Hints

Don't be afraid to try other items in place of shrimp: other shellfish, or even grilled chicken, sliced or diced
Also works with other pasta - rotini etc.

Serves - 4

Master Ingredient List

Penne w/Vodka, Tomato and Shrimp
1 lb. penne pasta

2 garlic cloves - peeled and minced
C. vodka
1 - 14 oz. can diced tomatoes
2 Tbsp. olive oil
12 large shrimp - peeled, deveined, tails off
Parmesan cheese to taste

Garnish
additional grated cheese

Wine Suggestions
2014 Layer Cake - Pinot Noir $14
2012 Domaine Gros Frere et Soeur Bourgogne Hautes Cotes de Nuits
    - Pinot Noir $34
2012 Clos Martinet - Proprietary Blend $55

Penne w/Vodka, Tomato and Shrimp
Bring pasta to boil, and simmer, covered for 10 min. until al dente

Sauté garlic, tomatoes and vodka in oil 10-15 min.

Add shrimp to sauté mixture 3 min. prior to serving

Toss sauté mixture with cooked and drained pasta

Stir in ½ of cheese with pasta/sauté mixture

Plate
Place a serving of mixed pasta centered on each plate

Garnish
Top with additional cheese to taste

Penne w/Vodka, Tomato and Shrimp

Time Line 1 hr.

Start 1 hr. before serving		30 min. after starting	Serve 1 hr. after starting
Vegetable Sauce 1 hr.	prep veg. 15 min.	cook down sauce 45 min.	
Veal 1 hr.	prep veal 10 min.	marinate veal 30 min.	cook veal 15 min.
Linguine 15 min.			cook pasta 15 min.+-

Cooking Hints

You can substitute chicken for the veal - slice chicken breast and then pound breast pieces until thin
You can easily omit the cream - just double the wine and reduce the wine sauce until thick sauce consistency

Serves - 4

Veal Scaloppini
1 lb. linguine

4 large or 8 small veal scallops - pounded to tenderize
1 C. white wine
½ C. flour - (can use gluten-free)
2 Tbsp. oregano
2 Tbsp. thyme
2 Tbsp. butter
2 Tbsp. olive oil
2 Tbsp. capers
2 lemons - zested (for garnish) and juiced

Master Ingredient List

Vegetable Cream Sauce
1 each - red, green, yellow bell pepper
   - cleaned and julienned
1 leek - cleaned, root end cut, up to green
   - 3" julienne
1½ lb. mushrooms - cleaned, stemmed,
   thinly sliced
2 Tbsp. butter
wine (from veal marinade)
1 C. chicken stock
1 C. heavy cream

Garnish
lemon zest and or additional capers

Wine Suggestions
2016 Justin Vineyard - Sauvignon Blanc $13
2016 Merry Edwards - Sauvignon Blanc $35
2014 Schieferkopf (Chapoutier) - Riesling $45

Vegetable Cream Sauce

Sweat vegetables in butter and olive oil

Strain sweated vegetables - reserving liquid and set aside - covered

Return liquid to saucepan, add stock and wine - reduce to ½ volume

Add cream and reduce to sauce consistency, add sweated vegetables

Season with salt and pepper to taste

Veal Scaloppini

Marinate veal in white wine for 30 min.

Remove veal from wine and reserve wine for vegetable sauce

Salt and pepper veal to taste and dredge through flour and spices

Sauté veal in a hot pan with butter and olive oil, each side 2 min.

Add capers to pan

Squeeze fresh lemon juice over veal at end of cooking

Linguine

Bring pasta to boil, and simmer, covered for 10 min. until al dente

Plate

Place a serving of cooked and drained pasta centered on each plate

Top with a serving of cooked veal

Top with vegetable cream sauce

Garnish

Sprinkle lemon zest and capers
   around each plate

Linguine Veal Scaloppini

Fusion Paella (Orzo) w/Curry, Coconut and Seafood

Time Line ½ hr.

Start 30 min. before serving	15 min. after starting	Serve 30 min. after starting
Orzo 10 min.+-		cook orzo 10 min.+-
Coconut Curry Seafood 30 min.	prep veg and seafood 15 min.	cook coconut curry seafood sauce 15 min.+-

Cooking Hints

You can use rice instead of orzo
Use any fish or shellfish you want.

Serves - 4

Master Ingredient List

Orzo
5 C. chicken stock
2 Tbsp. butter
2 C. orzo

Curry, Coconut and Seafood
1 - 4 oz. jar green curry paste
2 - 14 oz. cans coconut milk
1 C. white wine
2 onions - peeled and finely diced

Curry, Coconut and Seafood...cont.
2 garlic cloves - peeled and mashed
2 Tbsp. fresh ginger - skinned and finely diced
1 lb. each: mussels and clams
1 lb. any other seafood: squid, lobster, octopus, or shrimp
2 tomatoes - peeled, seeded and chopped

Garnish
dried cilantro

Wine Suggestions
2014 Lune d'Argent Clos des Lunes - Bordeaux Blanc $16
2015 Lewis Cellars - Sauvignon Blanc $35
2014 Ridge Estate Monte Bello - Chardonnay $55

Orzo
Bring stock and butter to boil in covered saucepan

Add orzo to boiling liquid, stir and cover

When stock/orzo boils again - reduce heat to medium (to keep the boil)

Boil for 10 min. +- or until tender

Drain the orzo and return to pot, covered

Curry, Coconut and Seafood
Heat curry paste in HOT, DRY pan (large enough for all ingredients)

Add coconut milk

Add wine

Add onions, garlic and ginger

Bring to boil

Add mussels and clams

Cook over medium heat until mussels and clams are cooked - 15 min.+-

They are cooked when the shells open - discard any that don't open

If using shrimp or other seafood that cooks fast, add these 10 min. before serving

At the end of cooking add chopped tomatoes and mix in with other ingredients

Plate
Place a serving of cooked orzo centered on each plate

Top with a serving of cooked coconut curry seafood

Garnish
Sprinkle dried cilantro over top of plates

Fusion Paella

Gluten-Free Fettuccine w/Green Chili Alfredo and Scallops

Time Line ¾ hr.

Start 45 min. before serving	20 min. after starting	Serve 45 min. after starting
Pasta 15 min.	cook pasta 10-15 min.	
Sauce 30 min.	prep veg. and clean seafood 15 min.	marinate scallops 5 min. and cook sauce and scallops 20-30 min.

Cooking Hints

Prep 15 min. Cook 30 min. Ready In 45 min.
Regular pasta and any seafood works too!

Serves - 4

Master Ingredient List

Gluten-Free Fettuccine
1 lb. gluten-free fettuccine

12 large scallops - rinsed
1 C. brandy
4 Tbsp. butter
2 Tbsp. gluten-free flour
2 C. skim milk

Gluten-Free Fettuccine...cont.
½ C. New Mexico Hatch green chili
1 C. part-skim ricotta cheese
½ C. grated Parmesan cheese
¼ tsp. salt
¼ tsp. coarsely ground black pepper
2 Tbsp. chopped fresh parsley

Wine Suggestions
2014 Bodegas Abanico Rioja Hazana Vinas Viejas - Tempranillo $15.
2010 Bernardus Soberanes - Pinot Noir $30
2013 Ramey Woolsey - Chardonnay $55

Pasta, and Green Chili Alfredo Sauce and Scallops

Bring pasta to boil, and simmer, covered for 10 min. until al dente

Marinate the scallops in the brandy - (reserve brandy when scallops removed)

Melt the 2 Tbsp. butter in a large saucepan over medium-high heat

Remove scallops from brandy and sauté in butter - remove when seared

Add 2 Tbsp. butter and flour to sauté pan, and cook for 1 min. stirring constantly

Add scallop brandy to flour butter mixture

Gradually add milk, stirring with a whisk until blended

Cook 15 min. or until thick, stirring constantly

Add New Mexico green chili

Stir in ricotta cheese, grated Parmesan cheese, salt and pepper

Cook 3-5 min. or until cheese melts

Add brandy marinated scallops and cook another 3-5 min.

Add cooked and drained pasta and mix well

Plate and Garnish

Place a serving of pasta, green chili Alfredo sauce and 3 scallops centered on
each plate, sprinkle with parsley and more grated cheese

*Gluten-Free Fettuccine with Green Chili Alfredo
and Scallops*

Pasta Carbonara

Time Line 1 hr.

Start 1 hr. before serving	30 min. after starting	Serve 1 hr. after starting
Pasta 15 min.	cook pasta 10-15 min.	
Bacon 45 min.	cook bacon. 30 min.	
Sauce 45 min.	prep veg. 15 min.	cook sauce and eggs 40 min.

Cooking Hints

Prep 20 min. Cook 20 min. - Ready In 45 min.
Regular or gluten-free pasta works for this.
Classic and rich - "eggs and bacon" pasta dinner!

Serves - 4

Master Ingredient List

Pasta Carbonara
1 lb. any pasta
1 Tbsp. olive oil

8 slices bacon, diced
2 Tbsp. olive oil
1 onion -peeled and chopped
1 shallot - peeled and chopped

Pasta Carbonara...cont.
1 garlic clove - peeled and minced
2¼ C. dry white wine
4 eggs - lightly whisked
½ C. grated Parmesan cheese
2 Tbsp. chopped fresh parsley
4 Tbsp. grated Parmesan cheese

Wine Suggestions
2014 Peter Lehmann Peter Lehmann Portrait Shiraz $13
2013 Tensley Syrah Tensley Vineyard - Syrah $39
2007 Paloma Palomita - Syrah $55

Pasta and Carbonara Sauce

Bring pasta to boil, and simmer, covered for 10 min. until al dente

Drain and toss with 1 Tbsp. of olive oil - set aside

In a large skillet, cook bacon until slightly crisp - drain and reserve grease

Heat 2 Tbsp. of bacon fat and 1 Tbsp. olive oil and heat in same large skillet

Add onion and shallot and cook over medium heat until translucent

Add minced garlic and cook 1 min. more

Add wine and continue to cook - 10-20 min.

Add cooked bacon to pan and add cooked and drained pasta - keep heat on

Toss to coat and heat through - if dry or sticky add more olive oil

Add beaten eggs and mix with tongs until eggs almost set

Add ½ C. Parmesan cheese and toss again

Add salt and pepper to taste

Serve immediately

Plate and Garnish

Place a serving of mixed pasta centered on each plate, sprinkle with parsley
and more grated cheese

Pasta Carbonara

Thai Dinner w/Peanut Dipping Sauce, Pad Thai, Green Curry Pork on Jasmine Rice, Ginger Crispy Fish

Time Line 3 hr.

Start 3 hr. before serving	45 min. after starting	1½ hr. after starting

Rice 30 min.+-

Pad Thai 2½ hr.	soak rice noodles minimum 2 hr.

Coconut Curry Pork 1¼ hr.	prep all vegetables - 30 min.

Ginger Fried Fish 30 min.

Sauce 30 min.+-

Cooking Hints

Here is a classic Thai dinner
The peanut dipping sauce is a great hors d'oeuvres and the Mango Salad on pg. 6 is a perfect starter
There are some good commercially available Pad Thai sauces that work well and save time

Serves - 4

Master Ingredient List

Peanut Dipping Sauce
2 Tbsp. oil
2-3 scallion - minced
2 garlic cloves - peeled and minced
2-3 chilies - minced
½ tsp. shrimp paste
¼ tsp. galangal (ginger)
1 tsp. tamarind
2 lemon leaves
1 C. peanut butter
8 oz. coconut milk
1 Tbsp. palm sugar - crushed to
    regular sugar consistency
cut veggies (small corn spears,
    broccoli, carrots, peppers

Pad Thai
8 oz. Thai rice noodles
4 Tbsp. fish sauce
4 Tbsp. lime juice
1 Tbsp. tomato purée
4 Tbsp. sugar
1 Tbsp. red chili pepper flakes
½ C. sake
½ C. vegetable oil
4 garlic cloves - peeled and sliced
1 lb. chicken - boneless/skinless, cubed 1"
8 large shrimp - peeled, deveined, tails off
2 eggs
½ C. ground peanuts
4 C. bean sprouts
1 bunch fresh cilantro - chopped

Green Curry Pork
1 lb. pork tenderloin - cubed 1"
¼ C. olive oil
2 garlic cloves - peeled and
    minced
1 large onion - peeled and diced
1 - 4 oz. jar green curry
2 - 14 oz. cans coconut milk
1 red bell pepper - cleaned
    and cubed 1"

Jasmine Rice
2 C. chicken stock
2 Tbsp. butter
1 C. Jasmine rice

Ginger Fried Fish
4 - 6 oz. white fish fillet
4 garlic cloves - peeled and minced
8 Tbsp. fresh ginger skinned and
    minced
12 oz. ginger beer
3 Tbsp. olive oil
2 limes cut in thin wedges

Wine Suggestions
Fetzer - Gewürztraminer $8
2004 Château Nairac - Sauternes $30
2013 Château Climens - Sauternes $69

Peanut Dipping Sauce
Sauté first 8 Dipping Sauce ingredients above
Then add:
1 C. peanut butter
8 oz. coconut milk
1 Tbsp. palm sugar

Heat mixture and serve with cut veggies (small corn spears, broccoli, carrots, peppers – red or green)

Jasmine rice
Bring stock and butter to boil in covered saucepan

Add rice to boiling liquid, stir and cover

When boils again - reduce heat to low and cook covered for 15 min.

Keep warm until serving

Pad Thai
Soak rice noodles in cold water for 2 hr. minimum

Drain immediately prior to using

Mix together next 6 Pad Thai ingredients (fish sauce mixture)

In a large wok (very hot) brown garlic in oil

Add chicken - sauté until just cooked - remove and set aside

Add shrimp - sauté until just cooked - remove and set aside

Add eggs and continue to stir fry

Add drained rice noodles, fish sauce mixture, stir fry for 3 min.

Add peanuts, bean sprouts and stir fry for 2 min.

Return chicken and shrimp to wok

Mix all ingredients well and keep warm until serving

...continued

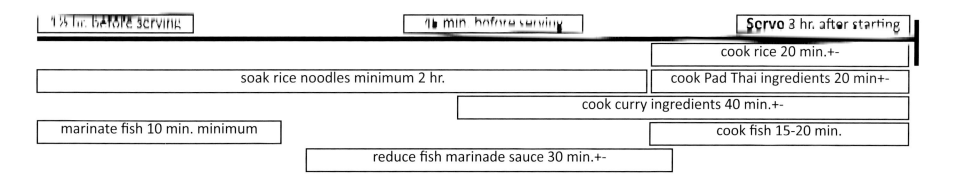

1½ hr. before serving		1 min. before serving		Serve 3 hr. after starting

- cook rice 20 min.+-
- soak rice noodles minimum 2 hr.
- cook Pad Thai ingredients 20 min+-
- cook curry ingredients 40 min.+-
- marinate fish 10 min. minimum
- cook fish 15-20 min.
- reduce fish marinade sauce 30 min.+-

Green Curry Pork

Sear pork pieces in oil in 4 qt. pan

When browned, remove and set aside

Sauté garlic and onion in same 4 qt. pan - until clear - 10 min.

Add green curry and mix well with sautéed garlic and onion

In same pot, add and bring coconut milk to a boil

Maintain boil for 10 min.

10 min. prior to serving add red pepper cubes and pork and
reduce heat to simmer

Ginger Fried Fish

Marinate fish in garlic, ginger and ginger beer for minumum10 min.

Remove fish from marinade 30 min. prior to serving

Add marinade to pan

Reduce marinade until sauce consistency 30 min. +-

15 min. prior to serving - heat oil to very hot and add fish - cooking
each side until brown and crispy - 5-10 min./side

Plate

Place a serving of rice on ⅓ of each plate

Ladle a serving of pork curry on top of rice - make sure to get all the
"stuff" in the curry on the rice too

Place a serving of Pad Thai on ⅓ of plate

Place a serving of crispy ginger fish on ⅓ of plate

Garnish

Top fish with marinade sauce

Sprinkle crushed peanuts and cilantro over plate

Place lime wedges around plate

*Mango Salad (pg. 6), Jasmine Rice with Coconut Curry Pork
and Chicken Shrimp Pad Thai*

Creme Caramel - Sunset and Caramel

Time To Prepare and Tips

Can be made up to one day ahead
Cooking in a bain means in a water bath - place the cups in a large baking pan filled with water - the hot water cooks the custard
To see "Painted Plates" watch the video on our website - **www.boozehoundsguidetogourmet.com**
For my painted plates, I use an ocean sunset concept with the plated creme caramel being the island on the water - you can paint anything!

Serves - 6

6 - 8 oz. custard cups
1 C. white sugar - to coat bottom of custard cups

Creme Caramel
¼ C. Grand Marnier or other orange liqueur
1 C. milk
1 C. heavy cream
3 whole eggs
1 egg white
¼ C. white sugar

Master Ingredient List

Creme Caramel...cont.
¼ tsp. nutmeg
¼ tsp. cardamom

Painted Plates
food color - red, blue, yellow
6 oz. white chocolate chips
6 oz. orange liqueur
4 additional custard cups or ramekins

Sugar Palm Trees
12 oz. white sugar - caramelized
large baking sheet
parchment paper to line baking sheet

Watch our "How to Paint Plates" video - http://www.boozehoundsguidetogourmet.com

Creme Caramel
Preheat oven to 375°

Heat 1 C. sugar in pan over high heat until caramelized

Pour caramelized sugar into custard cups - ½" in bottom

With beaters mix first 8 (Creme Caramel) ingredients

Fill custard cups with Creme Caramel mixture

Reduce oven heat to 300°

Place filled custard cups in "bain" and bake about 30 min. - then reduce heat to 200° for 30 min.

    (knife inserted in middle of cup should come out clean)

If you want more firmly cooked custard - maintain heat at 300° for 60 min.+-

Place cooled cups in fridge until need - up to 24 hr. is OK

Painted Plates
In a double boiler melt white chocolate chips and orange liqueur

When melted, divide into 4 - 8 oz. custard cups

Add drops of food color to each of 3 white chocolate/orange liqueur ramekins

In the 4th ramekin combine red and yellow to create orange

Using a paintbrush - paint the bottom half of a large white plate blue (the water)

Clean the brush in hot water between colors On the top half (blank) of the plate - paint alternating bands of red, yellow and orange -
    it's OK to have them blend together to form an interesting sunset

...continued

Painted Plates...cont.
Place finished plates aside and don't touch!

Sugar Palm Trees
Cover a baking sheet with parchment paper

Using a spoon - drizzle the caramelized sugar onto the
parchment paper to form a tree trunk and overhead
leaves

Allow to harden before handling

Plate
Place cooled creme caramel cups in hot water to melt sugar in
bottom

Dry warmed custard cup (so not to drip water on the painted
plate)

Run a knife around the perimeter of the cup

Place painted plate (centered) over top of custard cup and
invert holding plate and custard cup together

Lift custard cup off of plate to release creme caramel onto
plate

You may need to help custard fall out with a knife around the
edges

Garnish
Place Palm Tree in the middle of the custard (like a palm tree
on an island in the ocean in front of a beautiful sunset)

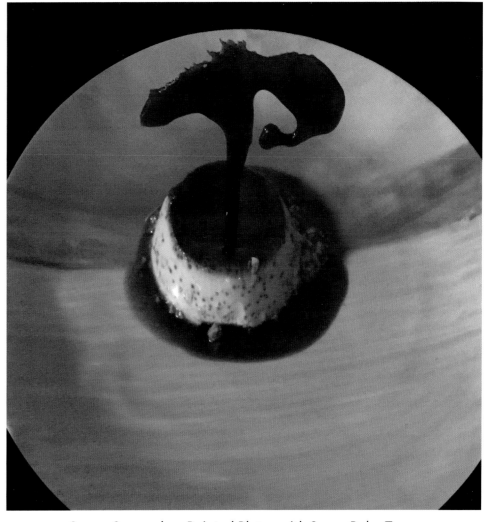

Creme Caramel on Painted Plates with Sugar Palm Tree

Trifle

Time To Prepare and Tips

Make one day ahead in a large trifle bowl
Prep 15 min.
Assemble, Cook and Refrigerate 4 hr.
Total time - 4-5 hr.

Serves - 8 to 10

Custard
5 C. milk
6 egg yolks
¾ C. sugar
½ C. cornstarch
2 tsp. vanilla extract

Trifle
1 small angel food cake
½ C. seedless raspberry jam

Master Ingredient List

Trifle...cont.
⅓ C. dry sherry
2 packages frozen, unsweetened raspberries,
thawed and drained
1 C. heavy cream
½ C. slivered almonds - toasted

Garnish
whipped cream
toasted almond slivers

Custard

In a heavy saucepan, heat milk until bubbles appear around edges

In a bowl whisk egg yolks and sugar until frothy

Mix in corn starch

Slowly whisk egg mixture into warm milk

Return to saucepan

Cook over medium heat, stirring constantly, until thickened

When thick, strain through sieve and stir in vanilla extract

Cover top with plastic wrap and refrigerate for at least 3 hr. -
(longer is better)

Trifle

Cut cake into ¾" slices and spread with the jam

In the bottom of a large, straight sided, clear bowl - spread a thin
layer of custard

Trifle...cont.

Place a layer of cake slice over custard

Sprinkle with ⅓ of the sherry

Dot with ⅓ of raspberries

Pour ⅓ of the remainder of the custard on top

Repeat above process 2 more times

Cover and refrigerate at least 2 hr. (or overnight)

Plate

Place a serving of Trifle centered on each plate

Garnish

Cover top of trifle with whipped cream and garnish with toasted
almond slivers

Chocolate Banana Pecan Cream Pie

Time To Prepare and Tips

Prep 15 min.
Assembly 15 min.
Total time - 30 min. + Refrigeration 60 min.
An awesome unbaked pie

Serves - 8 to 10
1 baked pastry shell

Chocolate Banana Pecan Cream Pie
¼ C. butter - softened
1 (3 oz.) package cream cheese - softened
1½ C. sifted powdered sugar
1¼ C. heavy cream

Master Ingredient List
Chocolate Banana Pecan Cream Pie...cont.
½ tsp. vanilla extract
3 bananas - sliced
1 - 6 oz. can pineapple juice
4 oz. dark rum
4 oz. chocolate liqueur

Chocolate Banana Pecan Cream Pie...cont.
½ C. chopped pecans - toasted
2 squares semi-sweet chocolate
1 C. heavy cream
3 Tbsp. sifted powdered sugar

Chocolate Banana Pecan Cream Pie
Beat ¼ C. butter and cream cheese until creamy

Add both powdered sugar and heavy cream in small amounts
        alternating with both - beginning and ending with sugar

Stir in vanilla extract, and set filling aside

Toss banana slices in pineapple juice and rum, then drain and pat dry

Spoon half of filling into baked pie shell

Arrange banana slices over top of filling

Top with remaining filling

Sprinkle with pecans

Melt chocolate in heavy saucepan over low heat

Add chocolate liqueur and stir well

Spoon melted chocolate into heavy ziploc bag and snip corner

Pipe ½ of chocolate (drizzle) over pecans and filling and set aside

Beat 1 C. heavy cream until foamy; gradually add 3 Tbsp. powdered
        sugar - beat until soft peaks form (for Garnish)

Cool in refrigerator for 1 hr. before serving

Plate
Drizzle leftover chocolate onto dessert plates

Cut pie into slices

Place a slice centered on each chocolate piped plate

Garnish
Spoon whipped cream into ziploc bag, snip corner and pipe dollops
        around edge

Chocolate Banana Pecan Cream Pie - the Whole Pie

Chocolate Banana Pecan Cream Pie - By the Slice

Limoncello Lemon Cake - *Ruth and Ernst Luthi*

Time To Prepare and Tips

Prep 15 min. Assembly 15 min. Bake 60 min.+- Total time - 1 hr.30 min.
Best made 1 day ahead so all of the glaze can soak evenly
You could easily increase the amount of glaze and over soak the cake - YUM!!

Serves - 4 to 6

Lemon Cake
9 oz. butter
1¼ C. sugar
5 eggs
3 lemons - zest for cake, juice for glaze
2½ C. flour
2 tsp. baking powder
1 pinch of salt

Master Ingredient List

Limoncello Glaze
½ C. powdered sugar
lemon juice from 3 cake lemons
½ C. Limoncello

Garnish
additional lemon zest
1 C. heavy cream - whipped with the Limoncello below
¼ C. Limoncello

Limoncello Lemon Cake

Whip butter and sugar to a foamy consistency

Add 5 eggs and the zest of 3 lemons

Mix flour, baking powder and salt and incorporate into
the batter

Pour into a 9" springform, lined with parchment paper

Bake in a 350° oven for 60 min.+- - until toothpick comes
out clean

Let the cake cool in the form

Glaze

Mix lemon juice from the cake lemons, the limoncello, and ½ C.
powdered sugar

Perforate cake with a wooden skewer and pour this mixture
over the cake evenly

Plate

Remove form from cake

Cut cake, and place a slice, centered on each plate

Garnish

Sprinkle lemon zest over cake

Place dollop of Limoncello whipped cream beside cake

Limoncello Lemon Cake with Whipped Cream

Cranberry Pecan Bourbon Pie

Time To Prepare and Tips

Prep 15 min. Assembly 15 min. Bake 1hr.30 min. Total time - 2 hr.

Serves - 8 to 10

pie crust - frozen pre-formed or just made

Cranberry Pecan Bourbon Pie
4 eggs
1 C. sugar
1 C. agave
½ C. melted butter
2 Tbsp. bourbon
1 C. chopped Craisins or dried cranberries
1 C. pecan halves

Master Ingredient List

Garnish
pecans - toasted
dried Craisins or dried cranberries

Cranberry Pecan Bourbon Pie

Preheat oven to 325°

Combine above Pie ingredients and pour into
    unbaked pie crust

Cover edges of pie with tinfoil and bake 60 min.

Reduce temperature to 300° and continue baking
    until pie is set" - 30 min.+-

Plate
Place a sliced piece of pie centered on each plate

Garnish
Scatter a few toasted pecans and some dried
    cranberries around the plated pie

Cranberry Pecan Bourbon Pie

Time To Prepare and Tips

Prep time 15 min.+-
Baking time 45 min.+-
Total time - less than 1 hr.
This could be done with gluten-free flour

Serves - 8 to 10

Master Ingredient List

Walnut Apple Rum Cake
½ C. butter
1 C. sugar
1 Tbsp. vanilla extract
¾ C. flour
8 oz. cream cheese, softened
2 eggs
5 apples - cored, peeled and sliced

Walnut Apple Rum Cake...cont.
2 Tbsp. light rum
½ C. walnuts - chopped

Garnish
1 C. heavy cream
¼ C. dark rum
¼ C. walnuts - chopped

Walnut Apple Rum Cake

Preheat oven to 425°

Butter 9" springform pan

Cream butter and ¾ C. sugar in a bowl

Add vanilla extract and flour

Blend well

Add eggs and mix with beaters

Pour batter into buttered 9" springform pan

Mix apples with remaining sugar

Add rum and toss

Arrange apples evenly over batter

Top apples with nuts

Bake in oven 45 min.+-

Plate

Place a sliced piece of cake centered on each plate

Garnish

Add ¼ C. dark rum to heavy cream and whip

Top plated cake with whipped cream

Sprinkle walnuts over whipped cream topping

Walnut Apple Rum Cake Without Garnish

Shirley's Delight - *Olga McGuinness*

Time To Prepare and Tips

Prep time 15 min.+- Baking time 30 min. Garnish 5 min. Total time - less than 1 hr.
This is one of those "you won't believe what's in this" desserts!
Real simple and easy to ad-lib new items - have fun
This could be done with gluten-free crackers

Serves - 8 to 10

Master Ingredient List

Shirley's Delight
½ tsp. baking powder
3 egg whites
1 C. sugar
17 Ritz crackers - crushed
½ tsp. vanilla extract
½ C. chopped walnuts

Garnish
1 C. heavy cream
2 Tbsp. Frangelico
1 square bitter chocolate

Shirley's Delight

Preheat oven to 350°

Grease glass pie plate

Combine Shirley's Delight ingredients and mix

Place into greased pie plate

Bake 30 min.

Remove from oven and cool

Plate

Slice cooled Shirley's Delight and place a slice centered
on each plate

Garnish

Top each plated slice with whipped cream/Frangelico

Melt and drizzle, or shave chocolate on top of
whipped cream

Shirley's Delight with Frangelico Whipped Cream and Melted Chocolate Garnish

Pavlova

Time To Prepare and Tips

Each component can be made ahead and at separate times
Prep 15-30 min.
Custard Sauce time 40 min.+-
Meringue Bake time 1¾ min.+-
Total time - less than 2 hr.
Make sure your chocolate cups are a similar size to custard cups

Serves - 8 to 10

pre-formed chocolate cups - 1 per plate

Meringue
4 egg whites at room temperature
¼ tsp. salt
¼ tsp. cream of tartar
1 C. fine white sugar - NOT POWDERED!!
4 tsp. corn starch
2 tsp. white wine vinegar
1 tsp. vanilla extract

Master Ingredient List

Custard Sauce
first part
1 C. whole milk
1 tsp. vanilla extract
4 egg yolks
½ C. white sugar
second part
4 Tbsp. B&B (Benedictine & Brandy)
½ C. heavy cream

Heavy Cream Filling
1½ C. heavy cream
¼ C. sugar
¼ C. Grand Marnier or other orange liqueur

Garnish
1 C. blueberries
1 C. blackberries
1 C. raspberries
1 C. black Sambuca (to marinate above berries)
1 strawberry per plate - sliced and fanned

Meringue

Preheat oven to 275°

Beat egg whites, salt and cream of tartar together in bowl until the whites hold stiff peaks.

Add sugar a few Tbsp. at a time, beating until mixture is stiff and glossy

Beat in cornstarch, then vinegar and then vanilla extract

Butter and lightly flour large custard cups and gently fill with meringue spreading it higher around the edges and lower in the center

Bake for 1-1¼ hr. or until meringue is firm and lightly browned(It should remain moist inside

Remove from oven and cool

Custard Sauce

Pour milk into saucepan

Add vanilla extract and simmer 8-10 min.

Keep warm on low heat

Place egg yolks in double boiler

Beat with mixer until quite thick and pale - about 6-8 min.

Place saucepan with yolks over low heat and gradually beat in sugar

Continue to beat custard base on low heat 4-5 min. more

Drizzle warm milk into custard mix and continue to beat

Continue heating over very low heat 10 min. more - stirring with wooden spoon

Custard Sauce...cont.

Remove custard sauce to stainless bowl

Add B&B and mix

Add heavy cream and mix

Reserve in fridge

Heavy Cream Filling

Start whipping heavy cream

After cream Is partially whipped - slowly add sugar

Add Grand Marnier or other orange liqueur to whipped cream

Reserve in fridge

Plate

Flood plates with custard sauce

Place 1 chocolate cup in the center of each plate

Cut well cooled meringues from custard cups and place meringues into chocolate cups

Spoon whipped cream onto meringue

Garnish

Place Sambuca marinated berries into whipped cream

Decorate plates with sliced fanned strawberry

Scatter berries around plate

Pavlova - Meringue Filled Chocolate Cup, B&B Custard Flood and Black Sambuca Berries

Apple Brandy Charlotte

Time To Prepare and Tips

Prep 30 min.
Assembly 30 min. Bake 60 min, Cool 60 min.
Total time - 2½ hr.
Can be done gluten-free with gluten-free bread

Serves - 8 to 10

Master Ingredient List

Apple Brandy Charlotte
6-8 hard apples - peeled and cored, cut into
      1" cubes
¾ C. brown sugar
¼ lb. butter
1 Tbsp. cinnamon (or more to taste)
½ C. brandy
2 loaves thick bread - at least day old is best
½ lb. butter - melted

Glaze
1 C. orange juice
½ C. sugar
lemon zest from ½ lemon
½ C. Grand Marnier or other orange liqueur
1 C. finely chopped dried apricots

Garnish
1 C. heavy cream

Apple Brandy Charlotte

Preheat oven to 400°

Sauté first 5 ingredients until fairly thick

Cut crusts off of bread

Slice all but 8 slices of bread into 1½" to 2" strips

Melt 2nd ½ C. butter

Line bottom of a greased 9" X 3" springform pan with foil

Cut whole bread slices, enough to cover bottom of pan

Dip cut bread slices in butter, sauté lightly and place in bottom
    of pan

Dip bread strips in butter and completely line sides of pan

Pour sautéed apple mixture into bread lined pot

Cover top with fitted cut bread slices dipped in butter

Bake at least 1 hr. - or until bread is a golden brown

Let cool at least 1 hr. prior to serving

Glaze

Bring Glaze ingredients to a boil then simmer for 15 min.

Blend in processor and strain

Reduce until quite thick, reserve

Plate

Un-mold Charlotte onto serving platter

Pour glaze over Charlotte and slice

Place a slice of Charlotte centered on each plate

Garnish

Pipe whipped cream onto slice of Charlotte on plate

Blueberry Oatmeal Crisp - *Andrea Cohen*

Time To Prepare and Tips

This is a fast, tasty dessert - less than 1 hr.
This could be done with gluten-free flour

Serves - 4 to 6

Master Ingredient List

Filling
unsalted butter, for the baking dish
6 C. blueberries
½ C. granulated sugar
3 Tbsp. all-purpose flour
2 Tbsp. fresh lemon juice
¼ C. Amaretto
pinch of kosher salt

Topping
¾ C. packed light brown sugar
¾ C. all-purpose flour
½ C. old-fashioned rolled oats
½ C. toasted pine nuts
½ tsp. grated lemon zest
6 Tbsp. cold unsalted butter - cut into 1/2" pieces

Topping...cont.
¼ tsp. ground cinnamon
½ tsp. kosher salt

Garnish
ground cinnamon

Filling
Preheat oven to 375°

Butter a 2 qt. baking dish

Toss the blueberries, granulated sugar, flour, lemon juice, Amaretto and salt in a medium bowl

Transfer to buttered baking dish

Topping
Combine the brown sugar, flour, oats, pine nuts, lemon zest, cinnamon and salt in a separate bowl

Using your fingers or a pastry blender, work the butter into the flour mixture until coarse crumbs form

Scatter the topping over the blueberry mixture

Set the dish on a baking sheet and bake until the topping is golden brown and the filling is bubbling, 45-50 min. (40 min. for altitudes over 5,000 ft)

Let cool slightly before serving

Plate
Cut and scoop a serving of crisp onto center of each plate

Garnish
Sprinkle cinnamon on top

A Fresh Baked Pan of Blueberry Crisp

Flambé Bananas - *Lisa and Emily's Burn Down The House Bananas*

Time To Prepare and Tips

Prep 10 min.
Cook and flame 15 min.
Total time - less than 30 min
An all time, fast, impressive, favorite - Everyone loves flames in the kitchen!!

Serves - 4

Master Ingredient List

Flambé Bananas
½ C. butter
2 ripe bananas - peeled and cut in half lengthwise, then slice
        halves into long quarters
½ C. brown sugar
1 C. dark rum
2 Tbsp. cinnamon
vanilla ice cream - the best quality you can find

A Pan of Flambé Bananas - Burning Off the Rum

Flambé Bananas

Melt butter in large saucepan

Add 1 Tbsp. cinnamon

Add brown sugar

Add the rest of the cinnamon

Add rum and allow to boil

Add bananas - sauté

While the pan is quite hot
Carefully - touch open flame to outer edge of pan
        IT WILL FLAME UP SO BE CAREFUL

Allow flame to burn out

Reduce pan liquid for a further 3-5 min.

Plate

Plate 1 or 2 scoops of ice cream in the center of each plate

Spoon 3 or 4 banana slices on and around the ice cream

Garnish

Spoon sauce from pan over bananas and ice cream

Flambé Bananas on Vanilla Ice Cream with Cinnamon

Ursi's Santa Fe Chocolate Cake - *Ruth and Ernst Luthi*

Time To Prepare and Tips

Prep 15 min.
Bake 1 hr.
Total time - 1¼ hr.+-
This cake keeps well in the refrigerator for several days

Serves - 4 to 6

Master Ingredient List

Ursi's Santa Fe Chocolate Cake
7 oz. butter
7 oz. dark chocolate (about 50% cocoa)
1 C. sugar
6 oz. ground almonds or hazelnuts
6 large eggs
¼ C. chocolate liqueur (i.e.. Creme de Cacao)
zest of 2 oranges

Garnish
chocolate liqueur - 2 Tbsp./serving
whipped cream
red chili powder in a shaker

Ursi's Santa Fe Chocolate Cake
Preheat oven to 350°

Melt 7 oz. butter and 7 oz. of dark chocolate (about 50% cocoa) in a pan

Add 1 C. sugar, mix well.

Add 6 oz. ground almonds or hazelnuts

Add chocolate liqueur

One at a time, add 6 large eggs and incorporate well

Pour directly into a 10" cake form (lined with parchment paper)

Bake on the lowest rack in your oven at 350° for about 1 hr.

When you take it out of the oven the cake should still be slightly jiggly

This indicates a very moist center of the cake which is what you want

Take it out of the form after it has had some time to cool off

Plate
Slice cooled cake

Flood each plate with 2 Tbsp. chocolate liqueur

Place a sliced piece of cake on top of flood on each plate

Garnish
Add a dollop of whipped cream

Sprinkle red chili powder over plated Cake

Ursi's Santa Fe Chocolate Cake on a Chocolate Liqueur Flood,
with Whipped Cream and a Dusting of Red Chili Powder

Pears and Brie

Time To Prepare and Tips

Prep 15 min.
Cook 15 min.
Total time - 30 min.
This is another of those - tasty, quick, great looking dessert that's very easy to make
You can change or omit nuts - as you prefer

Serves - 4

Master Ingredient List

Pears and Brie
½ C. butter
⅓ C. white sugar
4 oz. Frangelico
1 - 15 oz. can sliced pears - drained and sliced in thirds
1 tsp. chopped nutmeg
½ C. chopped hazelnuts

Pears and Brie...cont.
8 oz. Brie - warmed to room temperature, cut
         into bite size chunks- leave skin on

Garnish
nutmeg

Pears and Brie

Melt butter in large saucepan

Add sugar and mix pan contents

Add Frangelico and allow to boil

Add pears - sauté

Sprinkle with nutmeg

Add nuts

Add Brie

When Brie starts to melt - REMOVE PAN FROM HEAT!

Plate

Place pieces of pear, cheese and several nuts centered on
         each plate

Garnish

Spoon sauce from pan over pears, cheese and nuts

Sprinkle nutmeg over plate

Pears and Brie with Hazelnuts

Chocolate Salami - *Paula Guido*

Time To Prepare and Tips

Prep 15 min.
Assembly 15 min
Total time - 30 min. + Refrigeration time

Serves - 4 to 6

Chocolate Salami
½ C. dried cherries, cranberries,
    or any dried fruit chopped coarse
3 Tbsp. Grand Marnier or other orange liqueur
4 oz. ladyfingers, or vanilla wafers (or similar) - chopped
1 C. chocolate chips, either semi-sweet or bittersweet

Master Ingredient List

Chocolate Salami...cont.
⅓ C. heavy cream
⅔ C. toasted nuts, pine nuts, pistachio, or hazelnuts
½ C. confectioners sugar
½ tsp. chili powder, more if you want more heat

Garnish
confectioners sugar
blueberries

Chocolate Salami

Combine the fruit and Grand Marnier or other orange liqueur in a small bowl

Microwave until hot, (not boiling) about 45 seconds; let sit until the fruit has softened and the mixture is cool, about 15 min.

Reserve 1 C. of chopped cookies

Process remaining chopped cookies in food processor to fine crumbs (you should have about ¾ C.)

Microwave chocolate chips and cream in a medium bowl at 50% power, stirring frequently, until melted and smooth

Add fine cookie crumbs to chocolate mixture and stir

Add nuts, reserved chopped cookie pieces and fruit mixture then stir until thick dough forms

Divide dough in half and place each half on a large sheet of plastic wrap

Use plastic to form a roll for each dough half into tight 6" log resembling a salami (you can make one roll if you choose) twisting ends well to secure

Refrigerateuntillogs are firm, at least 3 hr. (longer if you choose to make 1 large salami)

Wrapped dough can be stored in refrigerator for 3 days

When ready to serve, place confectioners sugar in a shallow dish

Unwrap logs and roll in sugar until coated, brushing off excess

Cut each log into ¼" thick diagonal slices

Plate
Place 3 cut pieces of chocolate salami centered on each plate

Garnish
Place several blueberries on each plate and sprinkle confectioners sugar over chocolate salami

Chocolate Salami with Blueberry Garnish

Tres Leches

Time To Prepare and Tips

Prep and mix 30 min. Bake 45 min. Cooling 2 hr.
Meringue and "wet" cake 30 min.
Total time - 2½ hr.
This is a traditional Mexican milk cake, made using tres leches (3 types of milk)
This takes some advance time, but once made can keep refrigerated for a couple of days
Great leftovers too!

Serves - 8 to 10

Master Ingredient List

Milk Syrup
1 - 12 oz. can evaporated milk
1 C. sweetened condensed milk
1 C. heavy cream
1 C. light rum
1 tsp. vanilla extract

Cake
2 Tbsp. butter (for buttering baking dish)
1 C. sugar
5 large eggs - **separated**
⅓ C. milk
½ tsp. vanilla extract
1 C. all-purpose flour
1½ tsp. baking powder
½ tsp. cream of tartar

Meringue
1 C. sugar
¼ C. water
3 egg whites
½ tsp. cream of tartar

Milk Syrup
Combine Milk Syrup ingredients until well mixed

Cake
Preheat oven to 350°

Generously butter a 13" X 9" X 2" baking dish

Beat ¾ C. sugar and 5 egg yolks until light and fluffy, about 5 min.

Fold in milk, vanilla extract, flour and baking powder

In a separate bowl - beat 5 egg whites to stiff peaks, adding cream of tartar after 20 seconds

Gradually add remaining ¼ C. sugar and continue beating until whites are glossy and firm but not dry

Gently fold whites into yolk mixture

Pour batter into prepared pan

Bake cake until it feels firm and an inserted toothpick comes out clean - 40-50 min.

Let cake cool completely on a wire rack

Un-mold cake onto a large platter

Pierce cake all over with a fork

Pour milk syrup over cake

Continue spooning the overflow back on top until all is absorbed

Repeat frequently until cake will hold no more liquid

Meringue
Place ¾ C. plus 2 Tbsp. sugar in heavy saucepan with water

Cover and cook over high heat 2 min.

Uncover pan and cook the sugar to the soft-ball stage, 6-8 min.

Beat 3 egg whites to soft peaks with cream of tartar in electric mixer

Add remaining 3 Tbsp. sugar gradually, continue beating to stiff peaks

Pour boiling sugar syrup in a thin stream into the whites and continue beating until mixture is cool to the touch

The hot syrup "cooks" the whites

Building the Cake
Using a wet spatula, spread top and sides of cake with a thick layer of Meringue

Refrigerate the cake covered at least 2 hr. before serving

Plate
Slice cake and place a slice centered on each plate

Garnish
Spoon any "leches" that has drained from the cake over top of plated slices

Quick Mousse

Time To Prepare and Tips

Prep 5 min. Melting chocolate 10 min.
Heavy cream and egg whites 20 min.
Total time - less than 30 min.
So easy! Works great as either a white chocolate mousse or dark chocolate mousse.
This looks great served in wine or martini glasses! Try other chocolate friendly liqueurs

Serves - 4 to 6

Quick Mousse
3 squares semi-sweet chocolate - white is good but dark will do
¼ C. Baileys Irish Cream Liqueur
6 egg whites
½ tsp. cream tartar
1 C. heavy cream

Master Ingredient List

Garnish
white or dark chocolate squares - opposite color of chocolate as used in Mousse

Quick Mousse
Melt chocolate and Baileys in double boiler

Whip egg whites until soft peaks form adding cream of tartar while whipping

Set aside

Beat heavy cream until thick

Fold melted chocolate into whipped cream

Fold egg whites into chocolate/cream mixture

Serving
Serve in wine or other fancy glass

Garnish
Shave chocolate over top - use opposite color of chocolate as used in Mousse - (white mousse/dark chocolate garnish)

Quick Mousse - White Chocolate with Dark Chocolate Garnish

Death by Chocolate Cake

Time To Prepare and Tips

*An outstanding, outrageous chocolate cake - like none you have ever had - takes hours though!! - **Count on at least 4-5 hr. to make this!**
A most intense cooking experience, but well worth the stress!
EQUIPMENT: measuring cups, measuring spoons, sifter, 9" cardboard cake circle, parchment paper, pastry bag with large star tip, double boiler, 4 stainless steel bowls (1 large), 2 whisks, 9" X 1½" cake pan, 12" serrated slicer, 2½ qt. saucepan, 9" by 3" deep springform pan, serrated knife, large metal spoon, cake spatula*

Serves - 10 to 12

Master Ingredient List

Cocoa Meringue
4 egg whites
⅛ tsp. cream of tartar
⅛ tsp. salt
1¼ C. granulated sugar
2 Tbsp. unsweetened cocoa - sifted
1 Tbsp. cornstarch

Chocolate Mousse
6 oz. semi-sweet chocolate - in ½ oz. pieces
1½ C. heavy cream
3 egg whites
2 Tbsp. granulated sugar

Chocolate Ganache
1½ C. heavy cream
3 Tbsp. unsalted butter
22 oz. semi-sweet chocolate - in ½ oz. pieces

Chocolate Brownie Layer
1 tsp. unsalted butter
1 tsp. all-purpose flour
4 Tbsp. unsalted butter
¼ C. all-purpose flour
2 Tbsp. unsweetened cocoa
1 tsp. baking powder
½ tsp. salt
3 oz. unsweetened chocolate - in ½ oz. pieces
2 oz. semi-sweet chocolate - in ½ oz. pieces
3 eggs
1 C. granulated sugar
1 tsp. pure vanilla extract
¼ C. sour cream

Mocha Mousse
14 oz. semi-sweet chocolate - in ½ oz. pieces
4 oz. unsweetened chocolate - in ½ oz. pieces

Mocha Mousse...cont.
½ C. water
4 Tbsp. instant coffee
2 Tbsp. cocoa, sifted
5 egg whites
2 Tbsp. granulated sugar
¾ C. heavy cream

Mocha Rum Sauce
6 oz. unsalted butter
1⅓ C. granulated sugar
1⅓ C. heavy cream
8 Tbsp. unsweetened cocoa - sifted
3 Tbsp. dark rum
¼ tsp. salt
4 tsp. instant coffee
1 tsp. pure vanilla extract

Cocoa Meringue Layer
Preheat oven to 225°

Trace a 9-in circle onto parchment paper using a cardboard cake circle and put it onto a baking sheet

Mix the 4 egg whites, cream of tartar and salt

Whip on high (using the balloon whip attachment) until soft peaks form - about 45-50 seconds

Gradually add 1 C. sugar while still on high

Continue to whip until the peaks are stiff, about another 1½ min.

Use a spatula to fold in and thoroughly combine the remaining ¼ C. sugar, 2 Tbsp. cocoa and 1 Tbsp. cornstarch

Fill a pastry bag with the cocoa meringue (if you have no pastry bag, fill a ziploc bag and snip off one of the corners)

Cocoa Meringue Layer...cont.
Fill the traced parchment circle with meringue

Start piping in the center and spiral outwards so that the whole circle is filled

Place the meringue in the oven and bake for 15 min

Then lower the oven temperature to 200°

Bake for 2¾ hr. min. more

Remove the meringue for the oven

Cool on a rack for about 45 min. before handling

Raise the oven temperature to 325°

...continued

Chocolate Brownie Layer

Preheat oven to 325°

Butter a 9" springform pan, coat it with flour, shake out any excess

Sift together ¼ C. flour, 2 Tbsp. cocoa powder, 1 tsp. baking powder, and ⅓ tsp. salt in a small bowl and set aside

Set up another double boiler

Place the 3 oz. unsweetened chocolate, 4 Tbsp. butter and 2 oz. semi - sweetened chocolate in the top half

Tightly cover the top with plastic wrap, heat for about 4½-5 min.

Remove from the heat and stir until smooth

Put 3 eggs, 1 C. sugar and 1 tsp. vanilla extract in an electric mixer

Whip on high (using the balloon whip attachment) until slightly thickened, about 1½ min.

Add the melted chocolate mixture to the egg mixture and mix on medium for 30 seconds

Chocolate Brownie Layer...cont.

Add the sifted dry ingredients and mix on low for 10 seconds, then on medium for 10 seconds

Add the sour cream and mix on medium for 5 seconds

Remove the bowl and use a spatula to thoroughly combine any unmixed elements

Pour the batter into the prepared care pan, spreading evenly

Gently bang it down on the table a few time to help level out the batter

Bake in the oven until an inserted toothpick comes out clean, about 35 min.

Remove and cool for about 5 min. and refrigerate for 15-20 min.

Remove the brownies from the fridge

Cut brownie in half horizontally - so that you have a top half and a bottom half - both of which are still 9" circle

Chocolate Mousse Layer

Begin preparing this while the meringue is baking and cooling

Heat 1" of water in the bottom half of a double boiler over medium heat

Be very careful to keep any moisture out of your chocolate while you are melting it, or else it will seize and be very difficult to work

Place 6 oz. of semi-sweet chocolate in the top of the double boiler and tightly cover the top with plastic wrap (do not allow the wrap to touch the bottom half)

Allow the chocolate to melt slowly, about 9-10 min.

Remove from heat and stir until smooth

Keep at room temperature until needed

Chocolate Mousse Layer...cont.

Place 1½ C. heavy cream in the well-chilled bowl of an electric mixer

Whip on high (using the balloon whip attachment) until peaks form, about 1 min.

Whisk 3 eggs whites in a large stainless steel bowl, until soft peaks form (about 3 min.).

Add 2 Tbsp. sugar and continue to whisk until stiff peaks form, about 2-2½ min.

Add a quarter of the heavy cream to the chocolate and whisk vigorously and thoroughly, then add it to the eggs whites

Now add the remaining heavy cream

Fold everything together gently but thoroughly and put it in the fridge until needed (for at least 2 hr.)

Mocha Mousse Layer

Set up another double boiler.

Put 14 oz. of semi-sweet chocolate, 4 oz. unsweetened chocolate, ½ C. water, instant coffee and 2 Tbsp. cocoa in the top half of the double boiler

Tightly cover with plastic wrap and heat for about 6-7 min. remove and stir until smooth

Put 5 egg whites in an electric mixer. Whip on high (with the balloon whip attachment) until soft peaks form, about 1 min.

Continue to whip while gradually adding 2 Tbsp. sugar

Whip an additional 30 seconds or so, until stiff

Whip ¾ C. heavy cream in a chilled stainless steel bowl until stiff

Mocha Mousse Layer...cont.

Fold a fourth of the egg whites into the melted chocolate mixture, then fold in the whipped cream

Fold in the remaining egg whites

Ganache Layer

Heat 1½ C. heavy cream and 3 Tbsp. butter in a 2½ qt. sauce pan over medium-high heat

Bring to a boil.

Put 22 oz. semi-sweet chocolate in a stainless steel bowl

Pour the boiling cream over the chocolate and allow to stand for 5 min.

Stir until smooth

...continued

Mocha Rum Sauce

Melt butter in a heavy saucepan over medium heat

Stir in sugar, heavy cream, cocoa, 2 Tbsp. rum and salt

Bring to a boil; reduce heat and cook 5 min. stirring occasionally

Remove from heat and stir in coffee granules, vanilla extract and remaining 1 Tbsp. rum

Cover and refrigerate

Let stand at room temperature 30 min. before serving

Assembly

Put a closed 9" x 3" springform pan on a baking sheet

Carefully place the top half of the brownie circle inside, topside up

Ladle 1½ C. ganache over the brownie layer

(If the ganache has solidified, put the bowl in a pan of hot water and stir until the correct texture is achieved)

Use a knife to trim off any of the cocoa meringue that got outside of the 9" circle you traced underneath it

Then peel off the parchment paper and very carefully place the meringue, top-side up, inside of the pan

Press down gently to eliminate air pockets

Spoon the mocha mousse evenly on top of the cocoa meringue

Place the remaining chocolate brownie half, bottom side down, on top of the mocha mousse

Chill the cake in the fridge for 1 hr, or in the freezer for 30 min.

Take out the cake and cut along the inside of the pan to release it

Pour the remaining ganache over the cake and use an icing spreader to spread the ganache evenly over the top and sides

Put the cake back into the fridge for another 10-15 min. to set the ganache

Fill a pastry bag fitted with a large star tip or use a ziploc bag with a corner snipped off

Pipe a circle of stars (each closely touching the other) along the outside edge of the top of the cage

Circle inwards until the cake is covered

Refrigerate the cake for at least 4 hr. (12 hr. is preferable) before serving

Plate

Run a serrated knife under hot water between each time you slice the cake

Flood each plate with 3-4 Tbsp. of the Mocha Rum Sauce

Arrange each slice of cake on a large plate (smaller servings will stand upright better and look nicer)

Grand Marnier Soufflé

Time To Prepare and Tips

Prep 15 min.
Bake 6 min.
Total time - less than 30 min.
There are 2 thoughts on soufflés - wet center and dry center - obviously the dry center takes longer to bake
Don't be afraid to play with baking time to find what suits your taste

Serves - 6

6 of 8 oz. ramekins

Grand Marnier Soufflés
4 oz. softened butter - to butter ramekins
4 oz. white sugar - to coat ramekins
7 eggs - **separated** – use 1 more egg than servings
½ C. white chocolate chips
¼ C. orange juice

Master Ingredient List

Grand Marnier Soufflés...cont.
6 oz. Grand Marnier or other orange liquor
2 tsp. finely grated orange peel
½ tsp. cream of tartar – for egg whites

Garnish
powdered sugar -
orange peel - julienned

Grand Marnier Soufflés

Preheat oven to 450°

Butter ramekins

Coat each buttered ramekin with sugar and shake out and save
    excess sugar for mixing into egg whites

In a double boiler - melt white chocolate chips and 3 oz.
    Grand Marnier or other orange liqueur

Combine egg yolks, softened white chocolate, orange juice,
    remaining 3 oz. Grand Marnier or other orange liqueur and
    grated orange peel

Whisk until just blended

Beat egg whites w/remaining sugar (from ramekins) and cream of
    tartar, until soft peeks form

Fold yolk mixture into egg white mixture

Spoon yolk mixture into ramekins - (fill them up)

Bake until puffed and browned - about 4-6 min.+—

Be very careful opening oven to look

Remove from oven, (VERY HOT - CAREFUL)

Plate and Garnish

Place (very hot) baked soufflé ramekin on middle of each plate

Sprinkle tops of each soufflé and plate with powdered sugar

Garnish with julienned orange peels scattered around each plate

Serve ASAP

Grand Marnier Soufflé with Julienned Orange Peel

Dairy Cake - *Andrea Cohen*

Time To Prepare and Tips

Prep time 15 min.
Baking time 1-1¼ hr.
Total time - less than 2 hr.
This is an old family recipe loaned to me by Andrea

Serves - 10 to 12

Topping
½ C. cocoa powder
1 C. granulated sugar
12 oz. semi-sweet chocolate chips
8 oz. walnut pieces

Master Ingredient List

Cake
4 C. all-purpose flour
2 tsp. baking soda
2 tsp. baking powder
2 C. granulated sugar
1 C. unsalted butter
4 large eggs
1 pint sour cream
2 tsp. vanilla extract

Topping
Mix cocoa, sugar, chocolate chips and walnuts together and set
    aside

Dairy Cake
Preheat oven 350°

Grease and flour a 10" tube pan

Sift flour, baking soda and baking powder and set aside

Cream sugar and butter until fluffy-about 2 min. with a standing
    mixer

Beat in eggs one at a time

Mix in sour cream and then the vanilla extract

Pour ⅓-½ of batter into tube pan

Sprinkle ½ Topping ingredients onto ½ batter in the tube pan

Pour rest of batter into tube pan and top with rest of cocoa
    mixture

Bake for 1-1¼ hr. until toothpick comes out clean

Plate
Slice cake and place a slice centered on each plate

Dairy Cake

Mascarpone Stuffed Poached Pears

Time To Prepare and Tips

Prep and assembly 30 min.
Cooking down the poaching liquid at least 1, maybe 2 hr.!
Total time - count on 3 hr.
Time consuming, but most of the time is cooking down the poaching liquid - turn on the heat and walk away.
Always a hit - dark, rich and super tasty! Will need a coring tool,and cheesecloth to wrap the spices in - the "bouquet garni."

Serves - 4

Master Ingredient List

Spices - the "Bouquet Garni"
¼ C. black pepper corns
6-8 cinnamon sticks
¼ C. cloves
cheesecloth to tie around the spices

Mascarpone Stuffed Poached Pears
4 ripe pears - peeled - stem on
1 gallon - jug red wine
1 C. sugar
8 oz. Mascarpone cheese - softened and in a piping bag

Garnish
powdered sugar in a shaker

Poaching the Pears

Make a "Bouquet Garni" of pepper corns, cinnamon sticks and cloves
   (spices tied up in a cheesecloth bag)

Slice (just) the bottom off the pears to make bottom flat

Place the jug wine, "bouquet garni" and peeled pears in large pot

Cover and bring to boil - continue to boil - covered for 30 min.

When pears are soft (knife goes in easily) remove from wine

Place pears upright on baking sheet

Remove bouquet garni from boiling wine and discard

Reduced Poaching Wine Sauce

Continue boiling wine until quite thick - another 60 min. +-

Add sugar to taste through the boiling reduction process

You want this to be thick sauce consistency and slightly sweet

Stuffing the Poached Pears

Slice stem and ¼" off top of poached pear and reserve stem top

Core poached pears all the way through and discard core

Place softened Mascarpone cheese in piping bag or ziploc bag
   with end snipped off

Pipe cheese into the cored pear - careful to fill but not burst pear

Place stem top back on top of Mascarpone filled pear

Plate

Flood each plate with 3 Tbsp. reduced poaching wine sauce

Place Mascarpone stuffed poached pear on center of wine flood

Garnish

Sprinkle powdered sugar over pear and spice wine flood

Mascarpone Stuffed Poached Pear

Chocolate, Pecan and Raspberry Strudel - *Paula Guido*

Time To Prepare and Tips

Prep 15 min.
Assembly 30 min. Refrigeration time 2 hr. minimum
Bake 30 min.+-
Total time - 3 hr. 30 min.
The strudels freeze well for up to a month in a freezer safe container without the confectioners sugar
Just thaw fully at room temp when ready to serve

Serves - 4 to 6

Strudel
3 C. flour
1 tsp. baking powder
7 oz. (Blue Bonnet only) margarine
3 tsp. sugar
⅓ C. vegetable oil

Master Ingredient List

Strudel...cont.
2 eggs
¼ C. milk
1 - 18 oz. jar of raspberry preserves (with seeds)
2 C. chopped pecans
12 oz. semi-sweet chocolate chips

Garnish
confectioners sugar

Making the Pastry

Preheat oven to 375°

To make the pastry: in a large bowl, mix flour with baking powder, softened margarine and sugar

Add oil and eggs and mix well

Add milk and mixuntilyou have a soft and consistent dough

You may need to add some more flour to achieve

Divide the dough into 2 equal parts and form into ball shapes

Wrap each ball in plastic wrap and refrigerate for 2 hr. or overnight

Roll out one dough ball on a lightly floured surface to make a rectangle about 11" X 16"

Spread about ½ a jar raspberry preserves, leaving a ½" border all the way around, top with ½ of the pecans and chocolate

Turn in the ends on all four sides and roll up in thirds on the longer side then lay seam side down on a parchment lined jelly roll

Use a cookie sheet without a rim to make it easier to cut the strudel

Repeat with the other dough ball

Bake for 10 min. then carefully slice into 1" slices with a sharp knife

Be sure to wipe the knife clean between slices

Bake 15-18 more min.

When cool, thickly dust with confectioners sugar

Plate

Place 2 chocolate, pecan and raspberry strudels centered on each plate

Chocolate, Pecan and Raspberry Strudel

Tequilime Pie

Time To Prepare and Tips

Prep 10 min.
Bake 15 min.
Total time - less than 30 min.

Serves - 8 to 10

1 Graham pie shell

Tequilime Pie
1 - 10 oz. can sweetened condensed milk
4 egg yolks
4-6 oz. key lime juice
¼ C. Tequila

4 egg whites - reserve for meringue (made prior to serving)
½ tsp. cream of tartar

Master Ingredient List

Garnish
lime slices - 2 or 3 per serving
grated lime peel

Tequilime Pie
Combine first 4 Tequilime Pie ingredients

Pour into pie shell

Meringue
Whip egg whites and cream of tartar until soft peaks form

Top pie with meringue

Torch top until meringue is lightly colored

Optional - bake un-meringed pie at 350° for 15 min. and then
top with and torch meringue

Plate
Place a slice of pie centered on each plate

Garnish
Place lime slices and grated lime peel on each plated pie slice

Tequilime Pie

Clafoutis - *Ruth and Ernst Luthi*

Time To Prepare and Tips

Prep 15 min.
Bake 60 min.
Total time - 1½ hr.+-
This can be made with pears also - substitute for pear brandy

Serves - 4 to 6

Master Ingredient List

Clafoutis
2 C. ripe cherries - sliced
2 Tbsp. cherry brandy
¼ C. sugar
1 C. milk
¼ C. sugar
3 eggs

Clafoutis...cont.
1 tsp. vanilla extract
¼ tsp. salt
½ C. flour

Garnish
powdered sugar
whipped cream

Clafoutis

Preheat oven to 350°

Combine cherries, cherry brandy and first ¼ C. of sugar in a bowl
and let stand for 30 min.

Butter a deep dish pie plate

Pour the liquid from the cherry/brandy/sugar mix into a
blender jar - set cherries aside

Add to the blender all of the remaining ingredients in the order
in which they are listed

Blend at top speed for 1 min.

Arrange cherries on the bottom of the baking dish

Pour batter over cherries

Place in center of preheated oven and bake for 45-60 min. or
until puffed and slightly brown

Cool to warm

Plate

Cut pieces from cooled/warm pan of clafoutis and place a piece
centered on each plate

Garnish

Sprinkle with powdered sugar

Place dollop of whipped cream on side of cake

Cherry Clafoutis with Whipped Cream

Chocolate Lava Cake

Time To Prepare and Tips

Prep 30 min. Bake 15-20 min. Assembly 15 min.
Total time - 1 hr.+-
Unfortunately, this dessert has very thin line between being under - and over - done. If the cake runs all over the plate you need to increase the cooking time. If the cake is hard and does not ooze chocolate, lessen the cooking time. If the cake does not come out then make sure the custard cup is well buttered and covered in the cocoa.

Serves - 6
6 of 8 oz. custard cups

Chocolate Lava Cakes
12 Tbsp. unsalted butter
½ C. unsweetened cocoa powder
6 oz. chocolate

Master Ingredient List

Chocolate Lava Cakes...cont.
¼ C. chocolate liqueur
3 large eggs
3 large egg yolks
½ C. sugar
1 C. flour

Garnish
powdered sugar in a shaker

Chocolate Lava Cakes
Preheat oven to 350°

Place sheet pan in the middle of the oven for at least 15 min.

Lightly butter six custard cups (6-8 oz.) and dust with the cocoa

Tap out the excess cocoa but make sure they are well coated

Combine the butter, chocolate and chocolate liqueur in a mixing bowl on top of a pot of simmering water

If you don't have experience melting chocolate then be very careful not to burn the mixture

Never melt chocolate directly over the cooking element

Heat chocolate mixture until melted and set aside to cool slightly

Beat the eggs and yolks and the sugar with a mixer on med/high speed for about 5 min. until they are thick & light yellow color

On low speed gradually add flour and then chocolate/butter mixture

Pour the batter into the custard cups filling them almost to the top

Place on the preheated sheet tray and bake for 15 min.

The consistency when done should be where the edges of the cake are firm and the top is still soft to the touch

Remove from the oven and let sit on a cool surface for 3-5 min.

Plate
Run a paring knife between the cake and custard cup to loosen

Invert your dessert plate over the custard cup (be careful, they're hot) and flip over

Tap the plate lightly and lift off the custard cups

Garnish
Serve with vanilla ice cream

Sprinkle powdered sugar over plated Lava Cake

Chocolate Lava Cake

Gluten-Free Bread Pudding Soufflé with Canadian Whiskey Sauce

Time To Prepare and Tips

Prep 15 min. Sauce 30 min.
Bake 20 min.
Total time - 1 hr.+-
An absolutely iconic dessert! This is classic New Orleans - wonderful and pretty easy!!
Some slight changes - Gluten-Free, Craisins instead of raisins and Canadian Club (slight bias here) instead of Bourbon

Serves - 6

6 of 8 oz. ramekins

Gluten-Free Bread Pudding
unsalted butter, for pan and ramekins
¾ C. sugar
1 tsp. ground cinnamon
pinch of freshly ground nutmeg
3 whole eggs
1 C. heavy cream
1 tsp. pure vanilla extract
5 C. gluten-free bread - crusts cut off, cut into 1" cubes
⅓ C. Craisins

Master Ingredient List

Soufflé
9 egg whites, room temperature
¼ tsp. cream of tartar
¾ C. sugar

Canadian Whiskey Sauce
1 C. heavy cream
2 tsp. cornstarch
2 Tbsp. hot water
¼ C. sugar
¼ C. Canadian Club

Garnish
powdered sugar in a shaker

Canadian Whiskey Sauce

Place cream in a small saucepan over medium heat and bring to a boil

Whisk together cornstarch and water; add to cream while whisking

Bring to a boil again

Whisk, then let simmer for a few seconds, taking care not to burn mixture on bottom

Remove from heat; stir in the sugar and bourbon

Stir until the sugar dissolves

Let cool to room temperature

Bread Pudding

Preheat oven to 350°

Butter an 8" square baking pan; set aside

Combine ¾ C. sugar, the cinnamon and nutmeg in a large bowl

Beat in whole eggs until smooth; whisk in cream and vanilla extract

Add bread cubes; stir, allowing bread to soak up custard

Scatter craisins in greased pan; top with egg mixture, which will prevent raisins from burning

Bread Pudding...cont.

Bake until pudding is golden and firm to the touch and a cake tester inserted in center comes out clean, 25-30 min.

It should be moist, not runny or dry

Cool to room temperature

Soufflé

Preheat oven to 350°

Butter six 6-8 oz. ceramic ramekins; set aside

In the bowl of an electric mixer, whisk egg whites and cream of tartar until foamy

Gradually add remaining ¾ C. sugar; continue whisking until shiny and thick

Test with a clean spoon

If whites stand up stiff, like shaving cream, when you pull out the spoon, meringue is ready

Do not over whip, or whites will break down and soufflé will not work

In a large bowl, break half the bread pudding into pieces using your hands or a spoon

...continued

Soufflé...cont.

Gently fold in a quarter of the meringue, being careful not to lose the air in the whites

Divide a portion of this mixture among the ramekins

Place remaining bread pudding in bowl, break into pieces and carefully fold in rest of meringue

Top off soufflés with this lighter mixture, piling it high, about 1½" over top edge of ramekins

With a spoon, smooth and shape tops into a dome over ramekin rim

Bake immediately until golden brown, about 20 min.

Plate

Carefully place hot soufflé centered on each plate

Serve ASAP

Garnish

Using a spoon at the table, poke a hole in the top of each soufflé and spoon the room-temperature Canadian whiskey sauce into the soufflés

Sprinkle powdered sugar over soufflé

*Gluten-Free Bread Pudding Soufflé
with Canadian Club Whiskey Cream Sauce*

Kirschtorte - *Ruth and Ernst Luthi*

Time To Prepare and Tips

Prep 15 min.
Assembly 15 min. Bake 30 min. + 1 hr.
Final Assembly 15 min.
Total time - 1-2 hr.
This torte can be made ahead of time and will keep covered with tinfoil for at least a week in the refrigerator
You will need 2 of 12" springform pans lined with parchment paper

Serves - 8 to 12

Master Ingredient List

Yellow Cake
3 large eggs
½ C. granulated sugar
1 tsp. vanilla sugar
1 C. all-purpose flour

Japonais Layers
3 egg whites
1 pinch of salt
1 C. sugar
4 oz. ground hazelnuts or ground almonds

Butter Crème
12 oz. unsalted butter (3 sticks)
2 C. powdered sugar
2 egg yolks
3 Tbsp. Kirsch (Cherry Brandy)
3 or 4 drops red food coloring

Kirsch Syrup
½ C. of water
4 Tbsp. sugar
½ C. of Kirsch

Garnish
powdered sugar
sliced almonds

Yellow Cake
Preheat oven to 350°

Mix eggs, sugar and vanilla sugar in a glass bowl

Put bowl in pan with hot water and mix with a wire whisk or electric hand mixer for 1-2 min.

Remove bowl from water bath and beat the mixture until a solid foam is formed

Add ½ of the sifted flour and incorporate carefully with a rubber spatula into the cooled foam, then add the remainder of the flour and gently mix

Pour mixture in prepared 12" springform which has parchment paper on the bottom and the sides greased and dusted with flour

Bake in preheated 350° oven for about 30 min.

Japonais Layers
Preheat oven to 250°

Beat egg whites with salt until stiff peaks form, add ½ C. sugar continue to beat to a silky shiny consistency

Fold in the 2nd ½ C. of sugar, but don't beat it any more

Add 4 oz. of ground hazelnuts or almonds and carefully fold it with a rubber spatula into mix

Have 2 springform pans of 12" diameter - bottoms lined with parchment paper

Carefully divide the mixture between the 2 pans and bake in the middle of the oven at 250° for about 1 hr. or until dry and lightly browned

Invert the baked bottoms and remove parchment paper carefully

Make sure this is done while still warm to avoid sticking

...continued

Butter Crème
Beat Butter Crème ingredients to a smooth consistency and let it cool in the fridge for a few min.

Kirsch Syrup
Allow water and sugar to boil until sugar is dissolved

Let it cool then add Kirsch

Assembly of Kirschtorte
Put 1 Japonais bottom on a plate of about 12" diameter

Slather about ⅓ of the butter crème evenly on it

Add the yellow cake on top and drizzle the Kirsch Syrup over it

Add the next ⅓ of butter crème on and top it with the 2nd Japonais bottom

Now use the last ⅓ of the butter crème to cover the entire cake

Garnish
Cover the sides with toasted almonds and powered sugar for the top

Designs can be done using a knife or other forms as desire

Sprinkle powdered sugar on top of Torte

Plate
Slice Kirschtorte and place a slice centered on each plate

A Slice of Kirschtorte

The Whole Kirschtorte

Alan's Macadamia Chocolate Tart

Degree of Difficulty 1/4

Time To Prepare and Tips

Prep 15 min. Assembly 15 min.
Bake 30 min.+-
Total time - less than 1 hr.
Real simple and real tasty
Feel free to change nuts to suit

Serves - 6 to 8

Master Ingredient List

1 ready made pie crust

Alan's Macadamia Chocolate Tart
2 eggs
1 C. sugar
¼ C. bourbon
½ C. flour
¼ tsp. salt
1½ sticks (6 oz.) unsalted butter - melted
6 oz. semi-sweet chocolate - chopped
2½ C. macadamia nuts (I use less)

Garnish
chopped macadamia nuts
chocolate square for grating on plate

Alan's Macadamia Chocolate Tart

Preheat oven to 400°

Whisk eggs, sugar and bourbon

Whisk in flour and salt, then butter

Stir in chocolate, pour into pie shell and cover with nuts

Press nuts into mixture in pie crust

Bake 10 min. then reduce oven to 350°

Continue baking until crust and nuts are golden brown

Plate

Slice tart and place a slice centered on each plate

Garnish

Sprinkle chopped nuts over plate

Grate chocolate over plate

Mixed Berries and Tequila Cream Sauce - *Tina Watterberg*

Time To Prepare and Tips

Total time - less than 15 min
Real simple and real tasty
Feel free to change fruit to suit

Serves - 6 to 8

Master Ingredient List

Tequila Cream Sauce
1 C. sugar (try confectioner's sugar to avoid granulation)
1 egg
1 stick butter (4 oz.) melted
⅓ C. tequila
1 tsp. fresh lime juice

1 C. each mixed berries - blue berries, raspberries, strawberries - cut to
     same size pieces as other berries

Garnish
2 Tbsp. lime zest

Tequila Cream Sauce

Cream sugar and egg.

Add butter and mix

Warm in medium saucepan until sugar is dissolved

Remove from heat

Stir in tequila and lime juice

Plate

Place mixed berries in shallow bowls

Pour tequila cream sauce over fruit

Garnish

Sprinkle lime zest over top of bowls

Derby Pie with Kentucky Bourbon - *Cathy and Kerr Terreberry*

Time To Prepare and Tips

Total time - less than 1 hr.
This is simply the easiest recipe to make
It can be made the same day you want to serve it, or refrigerated and served the next day

Serves - 8 to 10

1 ready-made pie crust

Derby Pie
½ C. all-purpose flour
1 C. granulated sugar
2 large eggs - lightly beaten
½ C. butter - melted
2 Tbsp. Kentucky bourbon
1 C. chopped walnuts
1¼ C. semi-sweet chocolate chips
1 tsp. vanilla extract
1 pinch of salt

Garnish
whipped cream or ice cream
chocolate for shaving or chocolate chunks

Master Ingredient List

Derby Pie - The Beginning

Derby Pie
Preheat oven to 350°

Combine the flour and sugar in a mixing bowl

Add the eggs and butter and mix to combine

Stir in the bourbon, walnuts, chocolate chips, vanilla extract
and salt

Pour the mixture into the unbaked pie crust

Bake for 40-45 min. or until the filling is set

Set the pie on a wire rack and let cool before slicing

Plate
Place a slice of pie centered on each plate

Garnish
Top pie with a dollop of whipped cream and shave chocolate
over top

*Derby Pie with Kentucky Bourbon, Vanilla Ice
Cream and Chocolate Chunks*

Cranberry Swirl White Chocolate Cheese Cake

Time To Prepare and Tips

Prep and Assembly 30 min.+-
Bake 60 min.
Total time - 1½ hr.+-
Best if made 1 day ahead and refrigerated
You can substitute blueberry for cranberry, fresh or frozen
You will meed a 9" springform pan for this dessert

Serves -   8 to 10

1 Graham cracker pie shell - crumbled

Cranberry Swirl
1½ C. cranberries - fresh or frozen
1 C. orange juice
½ C. sugar

Master Ingredient List

Cranberry Swirl...cont.
4 Tbsp. Grand Marnier or other orange liquor
1 Tbsp. grated orange peel
½ tsp. cinnamon

Garnish
remainder of Cranberry Swirl reserved for plating

Cheese Cake
12 oz. white chocolate
5 - 8 oz. packs cream cheese -
        warmed to room temperature
1¼ C. sugar
6 eggs

Cranberry Swirl

Combine Cranberry Swirl ingredients in saucepan and heat
    at medium until mix thickens

Bring to boil and stir occasionally - 8 min.+-

Transfer to processor and blenduntilsmooth

Reheat until thick sauce consistency - 15-20 min. more

Strain and reserve ½ for mixing and ½ for garnish

White Chocolate Cheese Cake

Preheat oven to 350°

Heat chocolate in double boileruntilmelted and smooth

Beat cream cheese in large bowl until smooth

Add sugar

Beat in eggs - 1 at a time

Gradually mix in melted chocolate

Grease 9" springform and wrap edges of pan with tinfoil

Place crumbled Graham shell into bottom and spread
    uniformly

Pour ⅓ cream cheese mixture into springform pan

Place dollops of cranberry mixture around springform pan

Add ⅓ of cream cheese mix on top of dollops

Place dollops around on top in places other than where
    previously placed

Add remainder of cream cheese on top

White Chocolate Cheese Cake...cont.

Repeat cranberry dollops - try not to place dollops over last dollops

With a knife - poke into pan and swirl gently throughout whole area of pan

Bake until edges puffed and golden - about 60 min.

Plate

Flood each plate with 2 Tbsp. cranberry sauce

Place a slice of cheesecake on the cranberry sauce

Cranberry Swirl, White Chocolate Cheesecake